SomaVeda®
Integrated Traditional Therapies

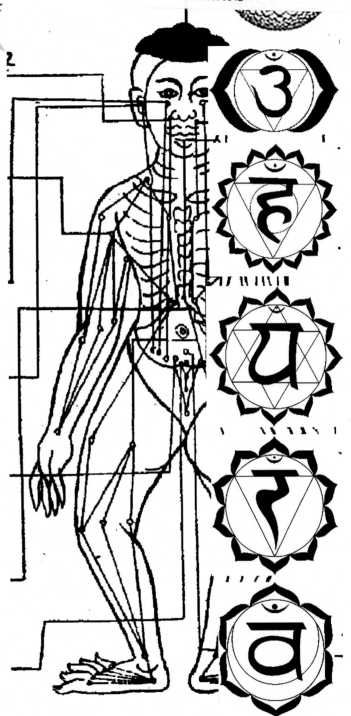

# Korosot

## Chakra
## Astrology

Psychology of Chakras for Yoga Therapy

By

Anthony B. James

*The eclectic and comprehensive introduction to the*
*SomaVeda® Integrative Traditional Therapies "Korosot" Chakra Astrology*
*method and The psychology of Chakras in human development and*
*classification of Korosot Chakra Body Types.*

# Korosot Chakra Astrology

## Psychology of Chakras for Yoga Therapy

By Anthony B. James

Inquires should be addressed to:

Anthony B. James
Metta Journal Press
5401 Saving Grace Ln, Brooksville, FL 34602
(706) 358- 8646

Published by Meta Journal Press
ISBN13: 978-1-886338-29-6

Printed in the U.S.A
Original art and photography, Anthony B. James
Color Chakra Panels, Original Chakra Art by Valentine Snow

ISBN: 9781886338296
52995

9 781886 338296

**Dedication:**

Thank you first to all of my teachers and those amazing individuals who first introduced me to the concept of chakras and the idea that they represented keys to understanding of our selves in ways not commonly possible. Thank you to my Ayurveda and Thai Nuad teachers and masters who showed me the way to using astrology as an intuitive assessment for the mental, physical and spiritual health of the client in front of me. I especially want to thank Aachan John of Chiang Mai Thailand who was such a happy and joyful teacher and master of Korosot, Aachan "Michael", the former Burmese monk who's stories of the "Old Days" of magic and medicine in the Golden Triangle held me enthralled, Aachan Phaa Khruu Anantasuk who taught me practical Korosot and the simple Thai way of getting to the pathways of incarnation used in Thai Ayurveda for centuries.

Thanks to all who supported putting this work out. My wife Julie who helped proof and fed me during the late night sessions on the computer and who said "Why not?" Valentine Vak Snow for contributing her energy and vision in the Chakra art and color plates. To everyone who helped edit, transcribe from lectures, or in any way or in any form of support to make this work public.

Aachan, Jon, Master Thai Korosot Astrologer, Chiangmai, Thailand 1989

# Thaat Thang Sii: Four Traditional Elements in Thai Ayurveda

The signals and information from the Chakra and Lom (Marma) system, mirroring the individual and composite planetary influences, completely determines our inclinations, moods, state of mind etc., or at least strongly influences our predispositions to react in certain and even predictable ways to every kind of event.

If you want to know what your mind was like in the past look at your body now. If you want to know what your body will be like in the future look at your mind now.

For ourselves, Korosot Chakra Astrology gives us the capacity to time travel. To go to a place where we can see ourselves more clearly in the past. To see how we got here and the trends of manifestation and events which formed and influenced our development and to see and perhaps positively influence the possibility of our future development.

For our clients, friends and family, it gives us the tools to quickly see a persons life, their attitudes and inclinations in perspective of their history. We can now see the current condition in which they find themselves as a triad of patterns of influence past, present and future.

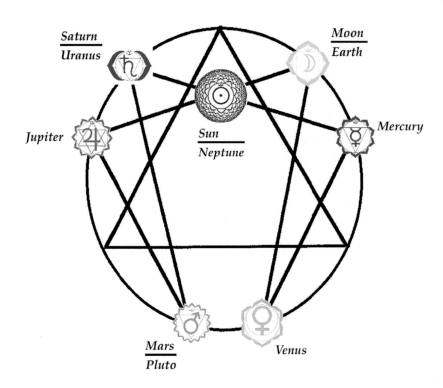

## Table of Contents

# Section One: Korosot Chakra Astrology

## What is Chakra Korosot?

SomaVeda® Korosot Chakra Astrology is a system of astrology based on the theory of Chakra and the the correlations we have found specific both to the individual Chakra and to the overall workings between all of the Chakra. These include more than 52 specific correlations including planetary, physical , psychological, mental, emotional, traditional archetypes, polarity, etc.

We are using two different approaches which we term "Standard" or Linear and Non-Linear.The linear is based on the typical or standard way of seeing and representing the seven primary chakra in a line, on the axis of the body and a progression of energy from bottom to top. We liken this to the observed chakra activity and physical manifestation.

In the Non-linear, we are using the Gurdjieff enneagram symbol as a model or prototype for the energy circulation and processes between the Chakra. (*Please note: In no way is my use of the enneagram symbol to be interpreted as an official representation of the Gurdjieff system*) The enneagram also give us a picture of the Chakra system as both a transformational system but a system that follows universal laws. It's planetary correlations give us the possibility to unlock the keys to the processes which the Chakra represent and to see our selves and the path of our lives in a different way.

Chakra Astrology like other more standard or traditional forms of astrology shares the hermetic theorem of "As Above, So Below." It is based on the esoteric understanding that we and the lives and consciousness we represent are not separate or distinctive from the universe around us. We in some way, or rather in many ways reflect the entirety of creation and the process of manifestation of creation within ourselves. The way energy works and circulates within us is the same as how it circulates in our solar system or the entire universe for that matter.

Chakra astrology primarily focuses on the influence of the nearest solar bodies or that of the planets of our solar system: Sun, Moon, Venus, Mars, Saturn, Jupiter and Mercury. Other typical astrology systems focus on the greater stellar sky and the 12 primary houses or constellations they represent. In Chakra astrology we are saying that we are living within the immediate "body" of the sun and as such are more strongly influenced by the influences, energy and if you will the consciousness of the Sun. It does not discount the influences of the extra solar universe and other systems it just emphasize a hierarchy at which the Sun is at the top of the influence pyramid and the individual planets representing literally the organs, the hand maidens of the suns
influence.

Since we are manifest in this environment ruled by the sun, literally everything about us from our physicality and body type to our emotions and psyche model or mirror the environment we are born into.

The Chakra system gives us an esoteric or hidden understanding of solar and planetary influences and their respective manifestations in our life. It is not chaotic. Just as there are regular laws of physics which the natural world conforms to there are laws of transformation which the natural world adheres to as well. The only difference between us and the universe is a matter of perspective, a matter of scale.

Additional considerations are found in the theories relating to the "Seven Step Ray of Creation". The soul seeks to manifest and does so as a composite of the twin influences of heaven and earth, celestial and terrestrial. This gives all the variety of higher and lower expressions of our consciousness.

There's a numerology expressed here. The most significant numbers are 1, 3 and 7. They refer to the laws, the Chakra, the Ray of Creation, the cycles of primary and secondary Chakra influence, the planets, the enneagram, conscious shocks and food necessary for conscious evolution and more.

One refers to the entirety, the Tao of everything, that which seeks to manifest. Three refers to the Law of Three or the three forces active, passive and reconciling which are the principles of creation and found in everything as well as defining each cosmos. Seven shows the interaction of higher and lower cosmos and how they relate one to the other.

By seeing these patterns and the logic of transformational processes we may have a hope , a possibility of participating in a more conscious way. The Chakra Astrology also gives us a new assessment tool to look behind the scenes of our lives for hidden patterns and influences both of positive and or negative polarity. If we can see these patterns then we might take the next step from simple observation to active participation in the process. Hopefully improving our lives by doing so.

Not limited as an assessment tool the Chakra Astrology then gives us a possible road map to that more conscious, that more positive outcome by giving definite directions as to what qualities need to be cultivated specifically to do this.

However, when used in a clinical setting, Korosot Astrology can be one of many good tools for assessment that one could use. It is a good counterpart and support for traditional Ayurvedic assessments such as Dosha, Pulse, Tongue, Iridology and Muscle Testing for starters.

# How Does Chakra Korosot work?

Refer to the Life Cycle of Chakra Influence chart. This is the linear cycle. Once you get it, it is going to jump out at you like crazy ball and make sense, but sometimes at the beginning, because it's new, it seems a little awkward for people to wrap their head around. But, it is logical and it is very, very simple.

First of all, across the top, we have the numbers one through seven. And in the corner it says "Peak Influence." But across the top of the chart, you see the numbers one through seven. Those numbers correspond to first chakra, second chakra, third chakra, etc. Now, look down the far left side of the chart. In bold print, it says "Individual Seven Year Cycle." So, we have 1/8; that's the first seven year cycle and the eighth seven year cycle. The next row says 2/9; that's the second seven year cycle and the ninth seven year cycle. 3 & 10, 4 & 11, 5 & 12, 6 & 13, 7 & 14, and then 1, starting at age 99, at the very bottom of the chart, would literally be the fifteenth seven year cycle. Basically, this is the potential age of an average person; ages 1 to 106 of your life are covered by this chart. Now let's go back and I'll break it down.

Starting at the moment of incarnation—your first year of life—you're in the first year of a seven year cycle dominated by first chakra. Additionally, the first year of that first seven year cycle, dominated by first chakra, is ruled by first chakra. So, if you drew a line across the page, that's the first seven year cycle, but then if you went top down, 1 to 1 or 1/1, we say, is the first year of the first chakra cycle. So, year one, your first birthday, is 1/1. Year 2—I'm now a 2 year old—is 1/2. In other words, it's still in the first chakra seven year cycle, but year number two is ruled by the second chakra. Year number three is ruled by the third chakra, etc. Year number eight is the first year in the second seven year chakra cycle. So eight is 2/1, fifteen is 3/1, twenty-two is 4/1, twenty-nine is 5/1, thirty-six is 6/1, forty-three is 7/1.

What if for example if your asking about an eight year old?

Step number one is to determine the age of the client. Once you know the age of the client, you locate the age on the chart. So, say your client is age eight.

Step number two, having located age eight on the chart, is to look at the left hand column and determine what individual seven year cycle that person is in. So an eight year old is in the second seven year cycle. But, that is ruled entirely by the second chakra, so in other words, all eight years (ages eight through fourteen) are ruled by second chakra. However, age eight is in the first chakra year of that seven year cycle, so it is 2/1. Second chakra is the overall, "big umbrella" principle for those seven years, but the year-specific influence is first chakra.

When they turn nine, nine is wonderful year, because it's 2/2; the diagonal line on the chart is what we call maximum energy. In other words, age one is 1/1. One and fifty, by the way is first chakra squared. Age fifty-eight is second chakra squared; so is age nine. So, nine year olds and fifty-eight year olds share something in common. One year olds and fifty years olds share something in common. Seventeen year olds and sixty-six year olds, twenty-five and seventy-four year olds, etc, all share something in common. They share the maximum squared attraction of the chakra energies for that year.

So, now you could pick any age. Tell me an age at random.

What if your asking about a forty two year old?

Find the age on the chart. What is it? Tell me the numbers.

(6/7)

So, it is the seventh year of the sixth chakra cycle. It is primarily ruled by sixth chakra or Ajna chakra, the chakra of the third eye. Go to sixth chakra, which is on page 77 and 78. Let's skip over to the qualities that we thought were important. So, for age forty-two, I want to look at the basic being, knowledge of being; look at the attributes of forty-two. First of all, the positive attributes, openness and objectivity. Distance and domination are the negative attributes.

Look at the quality, or the desire: clarity, union, unity, realization, intuition and revelation. We want to look at the primary activity of sixth chakra: transformation, transmutation. The nature is non-attachment and knowing. Now, while thinking about just the positive and negative attributes (openness and objectivity and/or distance and domination), looking at the desire, and looking at the activity, look at the person who's forty-two years old. They are at the end of the seven year cycle of some pretty severe, pretty strong growth. It is the peak year of transformation from the point of view of intuition, and development of knowledge and being as a person.

In other words from age thirty-six to age forty-two is the peak of influence of the sixth chakra. We've gone on a journey, in that the first year was about security and survival as it relates to 1) who I am in the world, my knowledge and being in the world, and 2) my transformational possibilities in life. So I've been through a journey by the time I get to age forty-two. And, after forty-two, I go back to security and survival mode and start over.

Another way of thinking about the seven year cycles is that these are the potential growth cycles of us in our consciousness and our being. We can be on track, we can be behind track, or we can be ahead of the curve. So, when I'm going to use this chakra astrology, and I have someone's age and I look it up and I see he/she isforty-two, and he's/she's in the last year of the sixth chakra cycle which is ruled by seventh chakra, it's all about transformation. But actually, what I'm going to do is go one year back. So, I'll look at 6/6. Wow, that was a powerful influence last year, at age forty-one. And, I'm going to look ahead at age forty-three, and I'm going to find out if it is a positive or negative trend. In other words, this year (now), is this individual positively or negatively aspected, what was he/she last year, and is there a positive or negative trend coming from last year and into this year?

From a counseling model, for example, I look at the information and determine the most positive things that this person needs to cultivate for next year. First, I look at the positive things that relate to the current year. For age forty-two, it is openness and objectivity, and if you're not cultivating that, you're behind, because you should already have that, you should already be working on that as your life lesson for this year.

Now I'm going to jump ahead to seven, and look at exactly the same thing. Look at purity of being; I'm going to look at extended and protected consciousness, flowing unobstructed as a pure and free manifestation of energy and light and transfiguration, and if you're negatively aspected now, I'm going to counsel you first to develop the positive expression that you should have now, which you don't have for some reason. I'm going to find out why you are not manifesting that, and then I'm going to counsel you to jump to the next step and cultivate the positive qualities of the next year ahead of time, and to reduce activities, and reduce whatever influences are in your life that are supporting the negative expression of the chakra, and also for next year, so that we can work on a model that not only will help have some correction right this minute, but will give you guidance for correction over time. So, I can use this as a three year model, past/present/future; that is how I do my trend in both psychological and emotional development, and actual lessons, actual exercises and actual work.

With this model, once you understand the chakras and the correlations with them, then you'll understand what parts of the body are emphasized, why there are trends in illness that happen in certain parts of the body, when they happen and why they happen, and there is a certain amount of prediction. For example, next year, you may need to really watch "X" part of your body, because according to this cycle, that area is going to be more vulnerable next year, as you see the trend developing this year. And, you can take more caution; maybe you need to work on cleaning up your diet, maybe you need to start exercising more, maybe you need to wear shoes when you're walking around outside because the feet are a weakness coming up next year. Maybe they're not; maybe it's your hands, maybe it's your mouth. It is whatever it is.

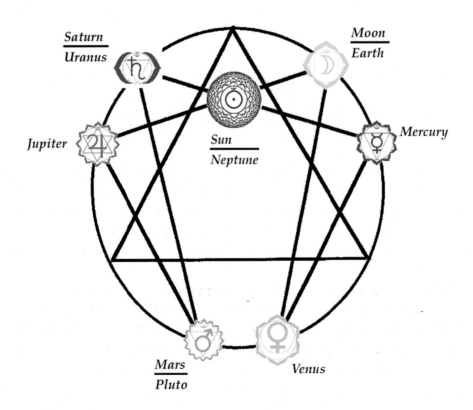

# Chakra Korosot Astrology for life guidance and personal growth.

I'm going to explain chakra astrology, or the principles of chakra astrology. Hopefully, in some semblance of a way that you are actually going to be able to do this very, very quickly. First of all, there are a couple of things that you need to have to do the chakra astrology: You have to have the chart, which has the life cycle of the chakras and the exact breakdown, and/or you have to memorize the chart. There are actually two kinds of charts. There is a linear and a non-linear chart.

**Please note:** this form of chakra astrology originated with me. This innovative astrology is not something that I was taught. This is actually something that I used my intuition to develop after studying the chakras for many years. That is why that Chakra Poster™ (Available at BeardedMedia.Com) is unique and nobody else has one like it; I invented it, I made it, I did the systematic development of it, and I've been teaching it for years and years.

First of all, the theory, when you study the chakras, is that we are all of the chakras, all of the time. All the chakras are active, all of the time. If any of the chakras were not active, you would be dead. You would just simply expire. It would be a broken link in that conscious chain between heaven and earth of the light force moving through you. If at any point that link is broken, you just made your transition. That is what it looks like. And that is what dying is. Dying is the release of energy from those doorways which anchor us to the present material manifestation of life. They are the anchor points that bring us into this place between heaven and earth. When we lose those anchors, there is nothing to hold us here anymore. And so off we go, like a balloon without a tether.

What we're talking about is the life cycle of the chakras in men and women. It follows universal principals, and I'll tell you how I got the idea for this. Actually, it is really easy. I'm still surprised that more people haven't caught onto it independently. First, number 40 on the [chakra astrology] chart corresponds to the ruling planet of the chakra. That is traditional. For example, the ruling planet of first chakra is moon and earth, or mother earth. The astrological symbols, however, are Cancer and Virgo. There has always been a traditional astrology symbol, or planet, that relates to the astrological sign or relates directly to the chakra. That is classic Ayurveda. So, there is a planetary correlation with every chakra, using the hermetic philosophy of "As above, so below."

I then realized that the planetary influences mean something. There is a correlation between the astrological significance of the planets, and the actual activity of the chakras within us. They are "same, same but different." The only difference between them is one of scale. I also realized that the planets go through cycles, and that we already know what these cycles are. Most of the major cycles are well known byastrologers or by anybody who studies astrology even just a little bit.

So, one of the things that I worked out was that there are seven chakras. I did confirm that; I surveyed approximately 150 sources, manuscripts and books etc. and pretty much confirmed that there are seven chakras. There are actually more than seven chakras—many more than seven—and that is agreeable with the idea of the secondary and tertiary chakras, which are not as important, but there are seven primary chakras. But, the other thing that I found was that these chakras, although they are all active all of the time, are dominant according to cyclical patterns.

The chakras change dominance according to cyclical patterns, and there are actually several different schemata, or several different ways, that the chakra dominance patterns manifest. I'll give you the first one. The basis of chakra astrology is the first and most obvious pattern. From the moment of your incarnation into this world, you are locked into a seven year cycle of chakra dominance. So, every year of your life, a different chakra is dominant, energetically, over your life - your body and physiology, your emotions, your psychology - and the next year of your life, you come into the role of the next chakra. It is the equivalent of a seven year Saturn return, except that instead of a seven year Saturn return, we have a seven year chakra return. In other words, we start with one, we end with seven, and we return to first chakra every seven years.

In my opinion, the only difference between the seven year chakra return and the seven year Saturn return is that a Saturn return can happen in a different year of life for different people. It is not related to your birth date. The chakra pattern is based on incarnation of energy. It is a seven year pattern that is based on when you actually incarnate in this life time. It is a different cycle from the Saturn return, so they don't overlap. In other words, the seven year cycle that is a Saturn return is another seven year cycle. We have more than one seven year cycle that occurs in our life simultaneously. They overlap, sometimes they build on each other, sometimes they're complimentary, and sometimes they are not complimentary. So, we have predictable strong cycles (upswing), predictable weak cycles (downswing). We have predictable cycles which are more emotional, predictable cycles which are more intellectual, predictable cycles which are more physical, etc.

Because I know the chart, I can draw it in my head.  So, all I need to know is your age. I already know what your life was like last year, I already know what influences are surrounding you this year, and I already know what's happening next year.

Now, here's the next way to know that. Remember, each of these chakras has a planetary correlation. So, for example, you can go to Llewellyn's publishing and get their yearly astrological calendar. In this chakra astrology, we're doing it year by year. In the advanced version of the chakra astrology, I can do it day by day. I can tell you the dominant influence of the chakras according to their astrology every single day. All I need to be able to do that is a good ephemeris that tells me the planetary aspects and their activity or dominance on a day by day basis. I mention Llewellyn's because they publish planetary aspects and ephemeris, and also softer calendars that just give the primary planets, their aspects, and what is the dominant planet each day. And so, you can be in any cycle, and on a given day you can have, for example, Venus as the dominant planet. Venus correlates to the second chakra, so when Venus is dominant, so is second chakra. So, you can actually break it down. You can do it simply like this. This is what I meant by it is the "short hand". However, should you choose to investigate further or to go into more detail, you can actually take it quite a bit further.

If you look back to first chakra on the Korosot chart. Look at the year/ number 50. Now you know what that is; that's the first column in the chart. So, you can just use the chart in general or you can memorize the ages.

You may notice that there are a couple of particular years that are actually delineated in this system that are pretty significant. When we turn 50, we've been through it all…And it's also two consecutive years that are in that diagonal of significance, back to back.

Forty-nine is a critical year, because forty-nine is 7/7 and fifty is 1/1.

Have you heard the term, "second childhood," or "mid-life crisis"? If you study this system, mid-life crisis jumps out off the page. Why? Look at the swing from the end of one cycle to starting the whole thing over again. And, you could actually say, if our longevity was what the ancients postulated that is was, we would even have three cycles in our life. So, we would have the first fifty years, as the Tamas, or we'd have our childhood which would last fifty years, we'd have our mid-life which would last fifty years, we'd have are elder's life which would last fifty years.

According to ancient Vedic literature, we were always meant to live 140-150 years. And so, we were supposed to be, at age fifty, just entering our maturity. That was the first mature state of life. It was the beginning of life. And here we are in our culture, and we think fifty, somehow is old. And we were always meant to be just starting our life at fifty, because the reason we can start is because we've completed our basic education, supposedly, on how to be a person, by age fifty, and then we start over, because that is what our energetic bodies support. And what happens, when you get to that point of transfiguration, and that point of transition, and you haven't completed the work? Now you're stuck starting over, with incomplete tools. And what does it look like? A train wreck.

A lot of people make their transition in their fifties; many people have crisis; there are a lot of divorces; there are lot of family breakups; there are lots of abandonment issues; lots of spending all of the family income on the new red sports car, there are a lot of people who become nuns in their fifties; Abandon life. Many people have inspiration also in their fifties. It's a very powerful year for both good and bad. The chart explains why. But actually, every year has a lesson and has an opportunity. That is one of the things you learn about the chakra cycles.

When considering the first seven year cycle, the first seven years is about security and survival. Basically, your objective, the first seven years of life, is to learn how to not get killed, either accidentally by yourself, or by someone or something in your environment. That is your job, so you can then learn what you need to learn the next seven years. For example, the job of a one year old is nothing but security and survival. They have no other interest in life. Eat, poop sleep. No matter how entertaining the baby may be, the primary life objectives are to eat, poop, and sleep. I know fifty year olds who are the same way. They might do some other stuff, but their primary life objectives are food, sleeping and their bowel movements. People get very, very concerned about their bowel movements in their fifties.

The second year of life is when the baby gets entertaining. The first year of life, the baby survived by staying close to the mother, and having a physical expression, and a phenomenal expression of chemical soup that attracts adults (the big eyes, the big head, the little body…all those features that make babies attractive). Then as they start looking like children, they're not so fun. When they're one year old and sometimes two, you say things like, "I could just eat you up." You want to just come over and grab a foot and start gnawing on it. Somewhere after two, that goes away. Also, a two-year-old might kick you in the face if you tried to bite his/her foot. Or he/she will bite you back. So, the two-year-old is all about personality. That is that second chakra kicking in. The personality is in such a way as to keep attention on them. And that's why they call it "terrible two's." It's a survival mechanism, the chakras built in survival mechanism to have them the center of attention, so somebody always knows where they are at, somebody knows what they are up to, and so they are in the inner circle. They're not left by themselves. They don't like to be left, even for a minute sometimes.

Then, in three years old, the security and survival of that first chakra influence, goes into the cultivation of intellect. Three year olds will argue with you. They don't have any idea what they are arguing about, no idea at all. But they are intellectually engaging. They want to challenge you and they want to interact with you intellectually. And that is another security survival strategy, because they have to start learning how to communicate. They have to start learning how to speak; how to say "I want, I don't want, I like, I don't like, feed me." But, they also need to mentally engage the adults around them. Why? They're getting bored, and they now need to start to stimulate the adults. The children need to stimulate the adults around them so the adults will find them more engaging and will want to stay closer to them.

Four year olds are nothing but love. Four year olds love you. Now the connection you begin to make with them is a deeper emotional bond, but it's not based solely on pheromones. There have been studies that show that the reason why mom and dad fall in love with the newborn baby is not because it is a newborn baby; it is because it smells funny. It is the actual pheromones that are in the afterbirth and that the baby actually produces in its brain and releases through its skin, and smelling the baby is actually what makes you love the baby. There have been studies that show if you isolate the parents from the baby where they cannot smell the baby, they do not develop the same emotional bond. But, that only lasts so long. Now we come into age four, and four year olds start having expression of their emotions in a heartfelt way. They are quite genuine. Four and five year olds, if they love you, you know that they love you. I'm simplifying, because it is so simple, that's why it's so powerful.

But, age five enters is into that communication expression of being. It might be in your favor, or it might not be. This will be determined by the environment in which your found. Does your environment, home, family, community support your development and expression as a person from a young age?

Six, again, is security and survival. All of a sudden intuition and reading between the lines kicks in. Now, all of a sudden, a six year old starts to discern that sometimes you don't always say what you mean and sometimes you don't always mean what you say. That is a survival necessity, because you have to be able to read people to be able to survive around people. You have to know when they are kidding or not. You have to know when they say, "Go run out in the street and play," that they don't really mean for you to run out in the street and play, because if you didn't understand that, you would run out in the street and get run over by a truck. And then they'd say, "What were you doing out in the street. You know you should never play in the street." And they'd (the child would) say, "Yah, but uncle Bob told me to run out in the street and play." By age six, they should be able to tell the difference. By age six, they are already studying the concept of lying. It is a survival skill. They know that everybody has to lie to survive. And that is when they start doing it. And that is when they start appreciating that when it happens (and they are imperfect in that); they start to develop this idea of being able to camouflage their emotions. They don't do it well though.

The seven year old is the end result of that first security and survival push. That is the master of the child. The grand master of babies is the seven year old. He/She is still a baby, but the grand master of the babies is the seven-year-old.

Eight-year-olds can have babies, biologically. In the last twenty years, several babies have been born to eight- and nine-year-old girls. Biologically, it's actually possible. What that means is even though they are immature - they are incomplete; they are not finished in virtually any function— biologically the body is already starting to mimic the adult body. So, eight years old is the first of the next seven years, which go from eight to fourteen. Do you know that in most cultures around the world, eight to fourteen was prime marrying years? In many countries in the world, they still make bride pacts and marriages for children between the ages of eight and fourteen. In many countries twelve to fourteen years is old enough to have a household, run a household, have children and be responsible for babies.

What is interesting here is that we think of the teenage years as going from maybe thirteen to, legally, nineteen or twenty-one, but from a chakra point of view that is not correct. From a chakra point of view, you've got a stage of maturity which is emotional from eight to fourteen, and you have a completely different set of ideas which is intellectual that come into play, and personality, and expression of personality that are not complete until age twenty-one, and so on.

Each stage is different but eight years old is the first year of that intermediate child. That is the child, not the baby. One through seven is the baby; Eight to fourteen is the child. So a fourteen year old is still emotionally undeveloped. But a fourteen year old is the master of the emotions of that range. Eight year olds are fitful, but if they're still throwing a fit at fourteen, something is wrong.

In other words, you can use this as a child development test. They should have mastered certain emotional development and expression by age twelve. And then, you look at ages fifteen to twenty-one. Historically, even in this country, it is only in our generation that fifteen year olds were not legally old enough to marry, to have their own family, and to work in factories, to be farmers and to be coal miners. My grandfather and my great grandfather both started working in coal mines between the ages of eight and twelve. My father first went into a coal mine when he was nine years old. He started working for money in a coal mine at age twelve. I'm from a family of coal miners. That our my family business. coal miners, underground people.

What about between the age of eight and fourteen?

By the time my dad was fourteen, he ran away from home and he joined the army. He had an uncle who lied about his age so he could get in. They lied and said that he was seventeen, and they believed him because he looked strong (because he'd been working in a coal mine since he was twelve). He had a demeanor of somebody who works hard, is strong and is very bright, so when they lied about his age, at that time, they weren't required to submit a birth certificate. Basically, they just had a family bible that they wrote the date in and an uncle who swore, and my dad went into the army when he was fourteen years old. By the time he was seventeen he was a first sergeant and a tank commander. Then, he was 100% disabled by the time he was twenty-one. All this life experience happened, before he got out of that third chakra phase of personality development. And that is where he got stuck, because emotionally, he never matured.

Whenever you have marriage contracts in that twelve to fifteen-year-old range, it is either a lower emotional kind of bonding, or it is no emotional bonding. It might just be financial. It's all about the intellect. It might be financial, or it might be political. They don't have the development that comes with the development of the fifth chakra (communication and expression of being); they don't have the development of the sixth chakra, which is based on knowledge and experience.

The seventh chakra, that first seven chakra cycle which kicks in around age forty-three. The idea is that we're not an adult, a completed transformational being; we haven't actually had access to all the energies in rotation that we need to be whole, complete individuals, until somewhere in our mid-forties. Obviously, that is why for people who are well adjusted, well educated, well experienced, when they hit those years, they are the most powerful years of their life. "Peak earners," they call them, because they have it all happening. All the cylinders are burning, all the wheels are rotating, they have skills, they have knowledge, and maybe they have some support. These are powerful people in these ages.

But, possibility exists there for transformation. That is why, for most saints and sages, and for people who become saints and sages, this is where their big transformation usually occurs. The Jesus story has him having his epiphany two cycles earlier, starting around age thirty-three, but if you think about it, the Jesus story works at age thirty-three because it's 5/5, which is a peak year for communication and expression of being. So, of course it is a perfect time for him to have started. And my guess is, with the training that he supposedly would've had access to by then, that the year of his instruction was chosen intentionally.

Just like when we have a PR marketing initiative and we're going to start our new marketing campaign the month before Valentine's Day, on Tuesday, at 4 o'clock, and we'll simultaneously come out on TV, newspaper, flyer ads and campaigns, and we're going to put up point of sales in all of the stores in all the Victoria's Secrets on Friday, two weeks before Valentine's day, and we're going to do it all together all at the same time…We have a campaign because we determined that is our window of opportunity for the most emotional reaction to be able to sell the most uplifting brassieres. In the past, people did things according to their most positive aspect of astrology. So, Jesus would have very easily had the skills and the knowledge to be able to know that by choosing to have his coming out, and really making big public scenes in that year of his life, would have significance for people who know about these things, because they would see that makes sense.

Three and fifth chakra cycles are very similar. Three is about cultivation and expression of personality. Five is about communication and expression of being. So the seventeen year old, virtually, can exhibit some of the same qualities, and as far as the communication, it could look virtually identical. The difference between them is that three is the same as five, but on a lower scale. When five comes rolling around, it is the same information, but having gone through the window of transformation of the heart.

But note: you could be a year ahead or a year behind on the scale. That is where it gets tricky. That is why we go three years; always look behind a year, and to the next year, to have that window. Also, if the person is consistently positively aspected, and if they're working on themselves, they're going to be ahead of the curve. So actually, you find certain individuals that literally might be a whole cycle ahead, or behind. There is this concept of being fixated that it is possible to get locked into a 1/1 cycle, for example. So, you have a fifty year old who gets locked into security and survival and never gets out of it. And then he/she just goes through emotional, intellectual, expressions of being locked in that cycle; we call that fixated, or even fractured.

What about age 82 relating to the triad consideration of past/present/future breakdown?

For age eighty-two, all there years are about communication and expression of being. 4 is the emotional part of that, 5 is the intellectual part of that, and 6 is the spiritual/intuition part of that. 6, 5 and 4 are the spiritual chakras; 3, 2, and 1 are the earthly chakras. So, age eighty-one to eighty-three is all spiritual. They are all ruled byfifth chakra; only the quality of influence changes from year to year. So, you'd have to go back and look at the qualities of what were important last year, or if you want to know next year, you'd refer to age eighty-three, go to sixth chakra and look at all the qualities (positive, negative, activities, etc.), and determine what that would look like if that was an influence on a dominant fifth chakra state. That tells you what the person is headed for. You have a potential negative and a potential positive. Always counsel them to move toward the positive qualities, no matter how they are currently aspected.

You have to be creative. You have to look at the qualities, study the qualities first, and then look at what you actually do in your life, find the connection between the qualities and what you actually do and what's actually happening around you, and then you have to be crafty and creative, use that sixth chakra function (remember, all the chakras are active all of the time, it's just relative dominance in activity) to craft what would be the chakra balancing things, interests, activities and qualities that you will cultivate for next year, and then start doing it now.

Don't wait until next year to start cultivating the positive qualities for next year. As soon as you are in this year, they are the antidote to the negativity that you have now, so you start cultivating that, and that could look like anything, a job change, relationship change, geographical change, financial change, artistic change, it could look like anything. Also keep in mind, the source for further information is to get a good astrology text and look at the planets. Look at what it means when Venus is dominant, when Mars is dominant, when Jupiter is dominant, etc. We've got a seven year planetary cycle and a one year planetary cycle that are overlapping. You have to play with this idea of primary influence and secondary qualifier. The primary influence is the seven year cycle. That's the big one. The yearly qualifier is the individual yearly influence.

Is it possible for someone to be "stuck" or stagnant in their development in one chakras influence? For example a person in a position of authority?

Yes, it is possible. It is even predictable in people who are not working on themselves. But, they will still be having those cycles. You might have to look and dig a little bit and see the evidence of it. Even if they still make choices because they are fixated in one concept.

For example, Homeland Security (security and survival) is all first chakra, but it feeds the others. It is a way to control emotions, a way to control finances, etc. And that is self-serving, but on an individual level those people are still going through the chakra cycles, but politically they might be emphasizing something like that. That is why there are all these expressions of why people respond so differently to great trauma. One group of people will want to attack, and kill everybody and let God sort it out. Another group of people will look, and say, "Well, how does this affect our community?" That is their first focus.

Another group of people will say, "How does this affect me and my interests?". Another group of people will be objective about it and ask, "What were the real causes? Even the bomber people had families who loved them, and mothers, fathers, brothers and sisters. What is the human element of this really about?" Another group of people would want to get to the original, fundamental cause of this problem, and find the political issues that are unresolved, the economic issues, and the philosophical issues that are brought to bear. Another group might ask, "What's the universe trying to tell us? What does this say about who we are in the world?" Another group might say, "It is an opportunity for transformation."

So there it is: seven chakra types, seven chakra cycles, all expressing and reacting to the same event, seven different ways. You can take the whole range of how people reacted to 9-11, and you can plot them on the chart, and find (generally speaking) what their first inclination was to react, based on where they are/were.

The signals and information from the Chakra and Lom system, mirroring the individual and composite planetary influences, completely determines our inclinations, moods, state of mind etc.,  or at least strongly influences our predispositions to react in certain and even predictable ways to every kind of event.

If you want to know what your mind was like in the past look at your body now.

If you want to know what your body will be like in the future look at your mind now.

For ourselves, Korosot Chakra Astrology gives us the capacity to time travel. To go to a place where we can see ourselves more clearly in the past. To see how we got here and the trends of manifestation and events which formed and influenced our development and to see and perhaps positively influence the possibility of our future development.

For our clients, friends and family, it gives us the tools to quickly see a persons life, their attitudes and inclinations in perspective of their history. We can now see the current condition in which they find themselves as a triad of patterns of influence past, present and future.

7: Solar Seven Year Cycle — Ages 43 - 49/ 92 -98

6: Saturn Seven Year Cycle — Ages 36- 42/ 85 -91

5: Mars Seven Year Cycle — Ages 29 - 35/ 78-84

4: Jupiter Seven Year Cycle — Ages 16 - 28/ 71 -77

3: Mercury Seven Year Cycle — Ages 15 - 21/ 64 -70

2: Venus Seven Year Cycle — Ages 8 -14/ 57 - 63

1: Lunar Seven Year Cycle — Ages 1 - 7/ 50 - 56

# Chakra Korosot Life Charts

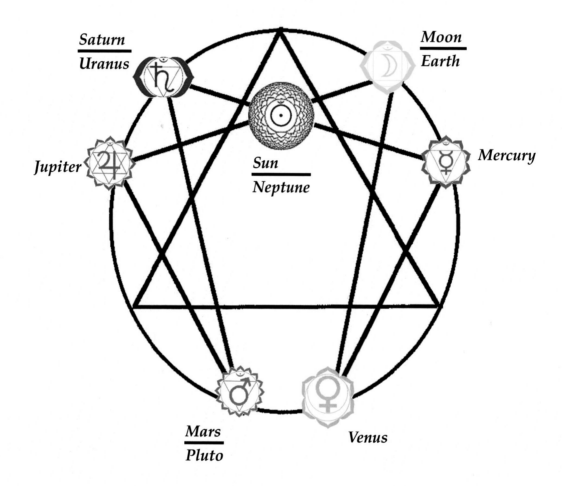

**Chakra Correlations with Planets**

# How To Use The Basic Chart

Years of double influence... Where the Principle and Sub yearshare the same Chakra.

> The first chakras first seven year cycle begins with year #1, The second chakras first seven year cycle begins with year #8.Each seven year cycle continues in turn. The first chakras second seven year cycle begins at year #50.

Individual Sub-Year of the Seven Year Cylcle

| Peak Influence | 1. | 2. | 3. | 4. | 5. | 6. | 7. |
|---|---|---|---|---|---|---|---|
| **1st. & 2nd.** 1/8 | 1 / 50 | 2 / 51 | 3 / 52 | 4 / 53 | 5 /54 | 6 /55 | 7 /56 |
| **Individual Seven Year Cycle** 2/ 9 | 8 / 57 | 9 / 58 | 10 /59 | 11 / 60 | 12 / 61 | 13 / 62 | 14 / 63 |
| 3/ 10 | 15 /64 | 16 /65 | 17 / 66 | 18 / 67 | 19 /68 | 20 / 69 | 21 / 70 |
| 4/ 11 | 22 / 71 | 23 / 72 | 24 /73 | 25 / 74 | 26 /75 | 27 / 76 | 28 /77 |
| 5/ 12 | 29 / 78 | 30 / 79 | 31 / 80 | 32 / 81 | 33 / 82 | 34 / 83 | 35 / 84 |
| 6/13 | 36 / 85 | 37 / 86 | 38 / 87 | 39 / 88 | 40 / 89 | 41 / 90 | 42 / 91 |
| 7/ 14 | 43 / 92 | 44 / 93 | 45 / 94 | 46 / 95 | 47 / 96 | 48 / 97 | 49 / 98 |
| **3rd. Seven Year Cycle** 1 | 99 | 100 | 101 | 102 | 103 | 104 | 105 | 106 |

The idea isto bring intentionality into cultivation of the positive energies and qualities of the procession... this includes those beginning whee the "Seat " of the chakra is set and the next or coming year.

1. First look at the Age of the client and locate them on the chart.
2. Determine the specific Chakra Cycle their age locates them in.
3. Determine the Chakra Sub-year within the Ckakra seven year cycle.
4. What is the Chakra influence throughout all cycles... i.e. "First chakra in the third cycle = years 15 and or 64... So you would say they are (3/ 1). "The first year of the 1st, 3rd. Chakra Cycle is age 15 or the 1st. Year of the second, 3rd. chara cycle is age 64".
5. Determine the Chakra influences of both the yer before and the year after to determine procession of energies and influences.
6. **Determine the planetary associations (correlation #40 on Chakra chart).**
   **Lunar = 1, Venus = 2, Mercury = 3, Jupiter = 4, Mars/ Pluto = 5, Saturn = 6, Sun/ Neptune = 7**

# Life Cycle of Chakra Influence
## *Linear*

**Individual Seven Year Cycle**

← **Chakra and Individual Year** →

| Peak Influence | 1. | 2. | 3. | 4. | 5. | 6. | 7. |
|---|---|---|---|---|---|---|---|
| 1/8 | 1 / 50 | 2 / 51 | 3 / 52 | 4 / 53 | 5 /54 | 6 /55 | 7 /56 |
| 2/ 9 | 8 / 57 | 9 / 58 | 10 /59 | 11 / 60 | 12 / 61 | 13 / 62 | 14 / 63 |
| 3/ 10 | 15 /64 | 16 /65 | 17 / 66 | 18 / 67 | 19 /68 | 20 / 69 | 21 / 70 |
| 4/ 11 | 22 / 71 | 23 / 72 | 24 /73 | 25 / 74 | 26 /75 | 27 / 76 | 28 /77 |
| 5/ 12 | 29 / 78 | 30 / 79 | 31 / 80 | 32 / 81 | 33 / 82 | 34 / 83 | 35 / 84 |
| 6/13 | 36 / 85 | 37 / 86 | 38 / 87 | 39 / 88 | 40 / 89 | 41 / 90 | 42 / 91 |
| 7/ 14 | 43 / 92 | 44 / 93 | 45 / 94 | 46 / 95 | 47 / 96 | 48 / 97 | 49 / 98 |
| 1 | 99 | 100 | 101 | 102 | 103 | 104 | 105 | 106 |

The Linear Life Cycle of Chakra influence is based on the standard progession of chakra circulation and in Korosot represents the outer, literal and physical world.

# Life Cycle of Chakra Influence
## *Non-Linear*

Individual
Seven
Year
Cycle

← Chakra and Individual Year →

| Peak Influence | 1. | 2. | 3. | 6. | 5. | 4. | 7. |
|---|---|---|---|---|---|---|---|
| 1. | 1 / 50 | 2 / 51 | 3 / 52 | 4 / 53 | 5 / 54 | 6 / 55 | 7 / 56 |
| 2. | 8 / 57 | 9 / 58 | 10 / 59 | 11 / 60 | 12 / 61 | 13 / 62 | 14 / 63 |
| 3. | 15 / 64 | 16 / 65 | 17 / 66 | 18 / 67 | 19 / 68 | 20 / 69 | 21 / 70 |
| 6. | 22 / 71 | 23 / 72 | 24 / 73 | 25 / 74 | 26 / 75 | 27 / 76 | 28 / 77 |
| 5. | 29 / 78 | 30 / 79 | 31 / 80 | 32 / 81 | 33 / 82 | 34 / 83 | 35 / 84 |
| 4. | 36 / 85 | 37 / 86 | 38 / 87 | 39 / 88 | 40 / 89 | 41 / 90 | 42 / 91 |
| 7. | 43 / 92 | 44 / 93 | 45 / 94 | 46 / 95 | 47 / 96 | 48 / 97 | 49 / 98 |

The Non-Linear Life Cycle of Chakra influence is based on the progression of the Gurdjieff Enneagram... This is a personal adaptation and not a representation traditional to the Gurdjieff system! It represents the inner and or secret world of energy and transformational process.

# THE

# THEORY

# OF

# CHAKRAS

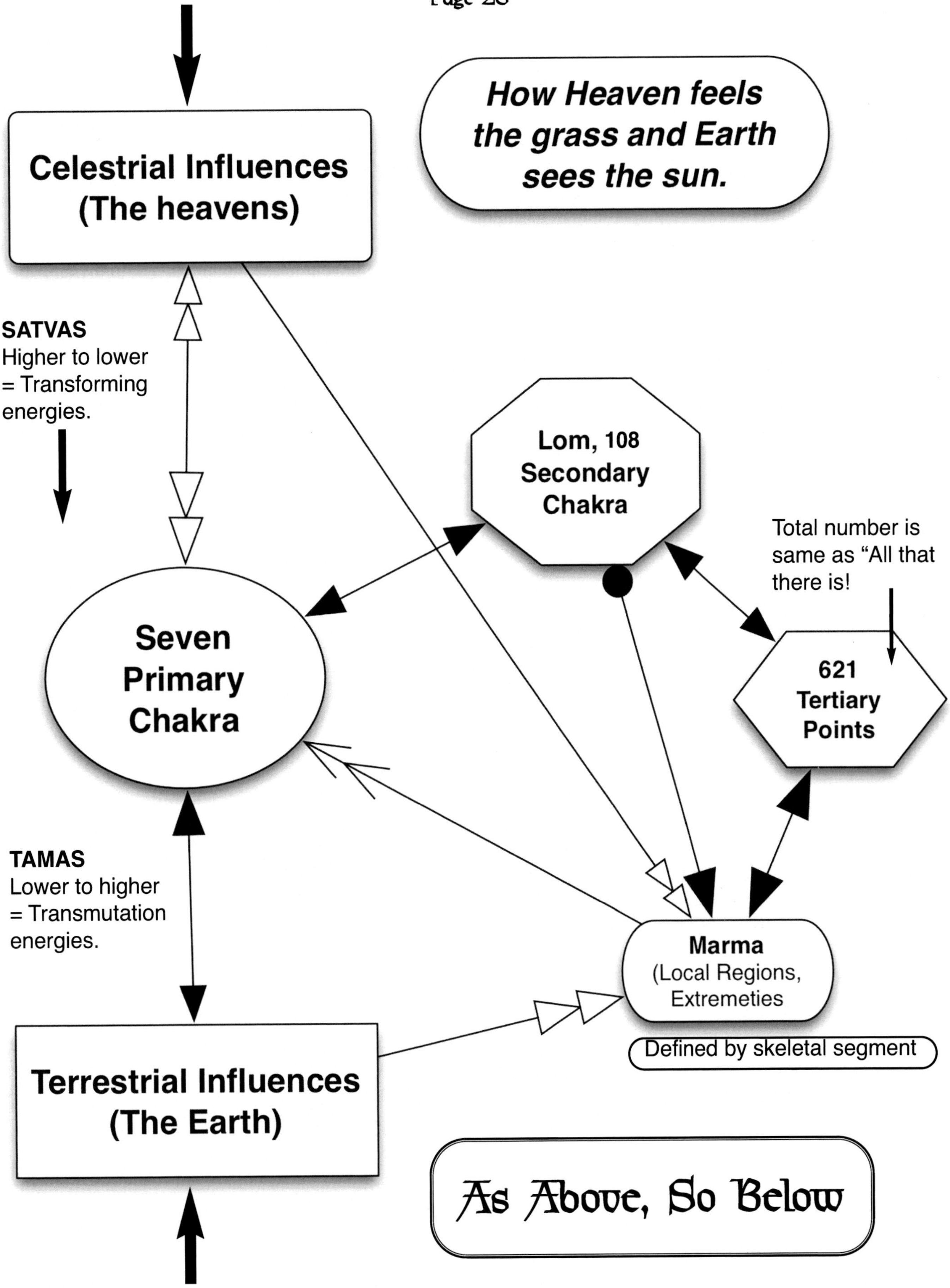

**Celestrial Influences (The heavens)**

*How Heaven feels the grass and Earth sees the sun.*

**SATVAS**
Higher to lower
= Transforming
energies.

**Lom, 108 Secondary Chakra**

Total number is same as "All that there is!

**Seven Primary Chakra**

**621 Tertiary Points**

**TAMAS**
Lower to higher
= Transmutation
energies.

**Marma**
(Local Regions, Extremeties

Defined by skeletal segment

**Terrestrial Influences (The Earth)**

As Above, So Below

# The Sevenfold Energetic Constitution of Man

The seven planes upon which man is said to have his being are listed as follows, from above downwards. The first or Divine plane; the second or Monadic plane; the third or Spiritual plane; the fourth or Intuitional plane; the fifth or mental plane; the sixth or Emotional plane; the seventh or Physical plane.

Each of these planes is subdivided into a further seven sub planes, giving a total of forty-nine planes in all. The highest aspect of man is found upon the monadic plane. This aspect uses the soul as its vehicle of expression, which is found upon the higher mental planes. The soul in its turn utilizes the lower self in order to gain experience in the three worlds of the lower mental planes and the physical plane.

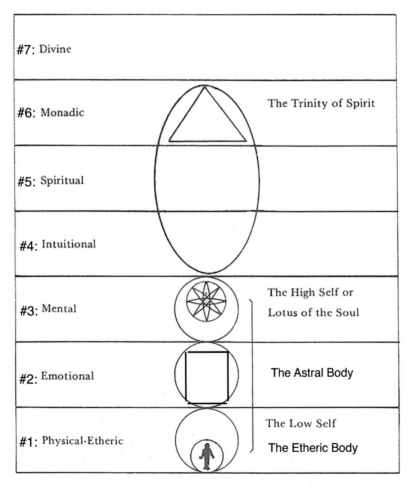

In other words man manifest as a trid of spirit, soul and body. The pure spirit is analogous to diety and celestrial influence or undiferintiated cosmic consciousness, the soul is the high self and the body the low self. The low self is likewise triple in nature, consisting of the mental body, the emotional or astral body and the physical/ etheric body. If we say the physical and etheric bodies are separate then the lower body is fourfold in nature. This may be an idea seen expressed in the four-fold square seen in the Yantra for first cahkra. The physical body may be the same as the physical body.

Previously, we saw how in traditional Ayurveda concepts that the person was made up of five Kosha or sheaths of the spirit. Once we start looking at the Chakra we are presented with another heirachy for the design of the body, one that is presented in seven aspectsor layers. These layers could be considered as overlapping and impinginging electrical or energetc fields or perhaps as a constant presented as a multi-diminsional concurrently existing phase state.

For practical application te practitioner will be primarily looking at the mental, emotional and etheric aspects, layers, fields or dimensions.

The menatal body is made up of mind stuff or Chitta. It is the more subtle of the bodies used by the soul.

The astral vehicle is that body through which emotion is experienced. The interplay of desire is felt in this body and for this reason it is sometimes called the desire body. Here are experiencedthe pairs of opposites such as pleasure and pian, fear and courage, etc. Most individuals are functioning very potently through this body, and as a result much disease stems from the constant chaotic interplay of energies within it. From the point of view of a practitioner focusing on energetic based healing methodologies it is important to ome to a fine understand of its workings. For example the SomaVeda™ B.E.T. tchniques are specifically focused to bring energy, awareness, consciousness and balance to the the astral body.

The etheric body, the densest of the subtle mechanisms vitalizes and energizes the physical body, and integrates the individual into the energy fields of the earth. The physical body, made up of the organic systems, comprised of dense, liquid, organic, mineral and gaseous materials, enables the souls a vehicle of expression in the physical plane or world of organic life on this planet.

Each or these layers of our constitution expresses energetically a picture of the equilibrium or health and well being of the individual. The discernment of these emanations and there states of energy tell the practitioner what is wrong with the client or at least what is most out of balance. The more the practitioner understands the energetic anatomy and physiology so to speak the greter the possibility of a being effective in in the art of healing.

All though all of the Chakra and "bodies" are active all of the time and working synergestically together, from an assessment and treatment point of view we want to focus on the disorders of the first and second and third chakra.

## FREQUENCY MODEL OF
## THE HUMAN SUBTLE BODIES

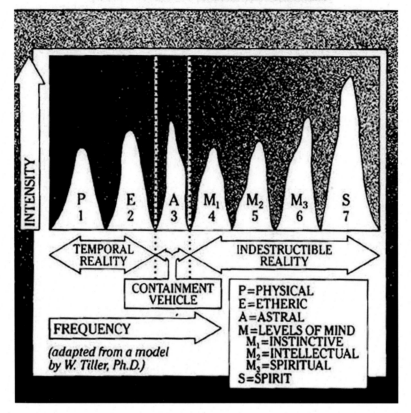

Diagram is from "Vibrational Medicine" page 156.

**Subtle Bodies and Healing:**   The 7 planes or subtle bodies surround and infiltrate the Physical Body in the following order: Etheric, Astral, Mental, Causal, Buddhic, Atman.  Each plane including the Physical is thought to have within it many dimensions.  Different healing modalities operate on different Bodies.  According to Gerber and others, specific kinds of remedies, rates and frequencies work by resonance with the specific disease miasms or parasites and engage the lower planes (Physical, Etheric, Astral and lower Mental), which Tansley warned us about.  Causal and higher modalities engage the Causal and Spirit Planes.  Such therapies include Crystals, Flower Essences and Oils, Gem Elixirs, Reiki and generally operate at much higher frequency ranges (TeraHertz) rather than at specific lower frequencies.  It seems likely that there are benign and toxic windows throughout the entire frequency spectrum which may fluctuate unpredictably. Frequent and repeated testing is thus extremely important, even several times, during a treatment session.  The idea of the seven planes easily correlates to the theory of Koshas, "Sheaths" or The five bodies as described in classical Ayurveda.

# Korosot
# First Chakra

# First Chakra: Muladhara Chakra
## ( Physical/ Physical) (Preparation )

It represents the earth, all of the earth. Literally manifestation into the physical, earthly life and all that that implies. It is the foundation of existence and being. The beginning and origin place of everything. All that follows contains within it the basic elements and compositions of constituents which originally manifest in first chakra.

To understand first chakra as well as the rest of the chkra, first consider that the chakras are a system of encoded numerology. Much of what we know of what the chakra system has to teach us is found in understanding, decoding and interpreting what the numbers and numerology depicted in various symbols mean. Numerology is not literally depicted intraditional symbols it is hidden in metaphor and geometry.

The form is a square to show the four corners of the globe, the four cardinal directions of the planet from the human perspective. These are the same as the four cardinal directions of North, South, East and West.

Four is a number which signifies completion i.e. 3 +1= 4.

The symbol or yantra of the chakra shows a circle and four petals (lotus petals). This is showing the four Sen or Nadi which are fundamental in this chakra; Sumana, Ittha, Pingkala, and Nanthakrawat. Please note that in the traditional descriptions, when ever petals are described they refer to specific Sen originating at that chakra.

There is a triangle to demonstrate the fundamental energy of kundalini shakti which arises from this point. Shakti refers to the principle of vital life force, agni, prana or chi. It is also a reference to the fundamental law of three. There are many "fundamentals" in first chakra. You begin to see why it is called the foundation chakra.

What is the "law of three" about? There are three forces of creation in nature. This ancient knowledge has been lost then rediscovered many times over the millennia. Let us discover it now for ourselves. The universe is created and ordered, otherwise chaos would exist, as opposed to order. The very idea of cosmos presupposes order distinct from chaos. This is the very foundation which leads us to hopeful thinking in reference to our own eventual "salvation" or enlightenment. Use whatever term suits your ears.

There must be at least three forces entering into every manifestation of energy. Creation is governed by the law and order of manifestation. Do not confuse this with ideas, man made concepts of law and order which change more frequently than the weather. This refers to certain immutable principles of great nature which are not dependent necessarily on our participation. We search for them in order to participate consciously as opposed to unconsciously.

These three forces have distinct and verifiable qualities. 1) Initiates, 2) Resists, 3) Balances and/or reconciles the first two. They are in man as they are in nature. All three must be present to create anything.

Third force is the Active force in the next triad. This reconciling force, is always the origin of a new triad. This process is self perpetuating and is the origin of life itself as a process. Think of the TAO expressed in concepts of Yin and Yang, which in moving about each other, give rise to a pivot or   reconciliation between them. Literally, the line between them becomes the first trigram of the I-Ching: Heaven, Man, Earth. From this begin ning comes all of creation to ten thousand things!  Heaven, Man Earth provides the continuum for all possible experiences of our world. Consider the Vedic concept of Prokruti and Purusha becoming the aggregates.

The Thai say the interaction of Nama and Rupa are the origins of defilements, progressively deteriorating our true perspective until nature is completely obscured. This distorted nature or the view of it is the world in its complexity. One triad begets the first force of the next and alll probabilities become possible in infinate variation. The Ayurveda Doshas or Bodytypes of Vata, Pitta, Kapha and Satvas, Rajas and Tamas exemplify this principle.

In the traditional depiction or symbolic representation of the Yantra or symbol for this chakra we find an elephant (Airavata/ Erewan i.e. the god of the heavens) with seven trunks. This is symbolic of the "Law of Seven" in nature and man.

Seven is the continuation of the law of three creating what is called an octave or seven step heirechy. It is two complete triads and the seed of the next at a higher or lower vibration. The first example of this would the " Ray of Creation", which begins with the absolute and ends with our moon, our line of creation. The Ray of Creation is a visualization tool to see the universal electrical fields which affect our own. These fields are not static and are in flux. The Ray of Creation illustrated here is worlds #1, 3, 6, 12, 24, 48 and 96.

**World #1**      The ABSOLUTE (What ever is the ultimate origin of everything)

**World #3**      World three, under three laws, 1st. level of creation, Galaxy, nebula, Black Holes etc., all possible systems of worlds.

**World #6**      World six, under 6 laws, our starry galaxy or our spiral arm of the Milky Way.

**World #12**      World twelve, our solar system, Sol or Sun's world. Our Sun may be in the greater orbit of a Black Hole in the center of our Galaxy along with millions of other solar systems.

**World #24**      The Planetary masses around the Sun, our solar system's organs and body if you will.

**World #48**      Gaia, the Earth, , where we live. Far from the absolute. See the veils that separate us. This is why this world is called Samsara, or ordinary world of suffering. Laws of nature: Earth Spin, gravity, tides, seasons, elemental forces, year and great year.

**World #96**      Luna, the Moon. We live on the earth. Now we see why the moon is a harsh  environment and a force to be reckoned with.

Common astrology deals with world's #12, #24 and #96 as they influence world #48.

Chakras are a model of this line of the Ray of Creation which passes through us. As above, so below. There is a chakra which resonates most clearly as an antenna with its representative world. All work on oneself consists in choosing the influences to which you want to subject yourself whether internal, external or both.

There are seven kinds of man and seven levels of mankind's development. Seven orders of influence over man and seven orders of intelligences which respond to man. Seven planetary cycles of seven different planets ruling our life and development. Seven Dhatus or constituents which make up the physical body. Seven colors in a rainbow and seven notes in a musical scale etc.

**Yoga:** The Yoga for first chakra is Hatha or Kundalini yoga. (Kalripayat and Martial Yoga/ Yang Yoga). Is Kapha Dosha.

**Proper Function:** First chakra is the lower, physical chakra. Origin of life, consciousness and the Astral body . Deep personal relationship to the earth and all life. Stable life and self esteem, balanced in harmony with natural cycles. Trust will be strong. Accepting out of your sense of security. Leads us to proper food, shelter and the necessities of survival and physical life.

**Disharmony:** Actions revolve around material world and possessions. There is no thought for tommorrows consequences. Hard to let go, constipation, overweight, easily irritated or upset, violence or violent thinking, especially enforcing will or control issues, rage and anger from lack of trust. No place is safe. Lacking physical or emotional stamina, worried, may not feel belonging to the earth, not grounded. May also lead to strategies of living which are actually contrary to longevity and survival. An example could be a drug addiction or crime or war etc.

**Balancing:** Sunrises and or sunsets. Sit on the ground while breathing up the essence of the earth. Sweats and or Sweat Lodge ceremony to engender entering  into the womb of mother earth in the community of all living beings.

**MULADHARA**
Sanskrit: मूलाधार
ROOT CHAKRA

1. **SYMBOL**
**First Chakra**

2. **COMMON NAME**
ROOT, Base, Origin,
Beginning

3. **SANSKRIT NAME**
MULADHARA

4. **INTERPRETED**
**MEANING**
FOUNDATION

5. **FORM**
SQUARE, Balanced, Faces
four directions

6. **TRADITIONAL**
**SYMBOL**
4 Petaled Lotus
facing up, Origin of Four
Sen

7. **COLOR**
YELLOW & RED

8. **LOCATION on the**
**SURFACE of the body**
Base of the spine, Facing
down

9. **LOCATION on the SPINE**
4th Sacral vertebrae

10. **PREDOMINATE SENSE**
SMELL

11. **SENSE ORGAN**
NOSE

12. **WORK ORGAN**
ANUS/ RECTUM

13. **ASSOCIATED GLANDS**
PANCREAS

14. **FUNCTION of**
**ASSOCIATED GLANDS**
Digestion, Lymphatic,
System, Insulin, Rules
Nutrition

15. **SYMPATHETIC NERVE**
**PLEXUS**
COCCYGEAL

16. **CHIEF**
**SUBSIDIARY PARTS**
Legs and Feet, Genitals,
Coccyx, Bones, Teeth,
Colon, Prostrate, Blood
and Hair

17. **MANTRA**
LANG / LAM

18. **VOWEL SOUND**
"OOH" , as in "Pooh", in
lower Key of C

19. **MUSIC THERAPY**
DREAMLIKE, Elfin,
Mysterious, Disturbing,
Drums, Repetitive and
Natural Rhythms

20. **EXAMPLES**
Clair de lune (Debussy),
La Valse (Ravel),
Symphanie Pathertique
(Tchaikousky)

21. **SUITABLE EFFECTS**
**and/or INSTRUMENTS**
DRUMS, Cymbals,
Delicate bells, Gourd
Rattles, Flute, Triangle,
Harp, Wind Chime, Night
Voices of Nature

22. **MUDRA**
Palm Down

23. **ELEMENT**
EARTH

24. **QUALITY OF THE**
**ELEMENT**
PATIENCE

25. **BASIC BEING**
PHYSICAL Being

26. **ATTRIBUTE**
**Positive/ Negative**
PATIENCE / GREED
Persistence / Resistance

27. **DESIRE**
SURVIVAL, Security, Food
and Shelter

28. **ACTIVITY**
COLLECTING and
Saving

29. **NATURE**
STABLE

30. **QUALITIES OF DESIGN**
CIRCULAR, Elliptical,
Maze Like Forms,

31. **RESULT of Unsatisfied Karma, To be Reborn as:**
NATURAL MAN,
Ordinary Person

32. **LOKA, Plane of Existence**
BHU LOKA, Physical

33. **VAYU, Type and Color of Vital Air**
APANA / VYANA
Orange / Red

34. **HINDU DEITY**
BRAHMA, Lord of
Creation, Krishna

35. **GREEK DEITY**
ARTEMIS, Selene, Hectate

36. **ROMAN DEITY**
DIANA

37. **ETRUSCAN DEITY**
TIVIS

38. **BABYLONIAN DEITY**
SIN, Zu-en, Nannar

39. **EGYPTIAN DEITY**
KHONSU (Nefer-hotep),
Ta-urt (Taueret), Gep

40. **RULING PLANET Symbol**
MOON / Earth, (Lunar tides &
Menses, Mother Earth)

41. **ASTROLOGICAL SIGN Symbol**
CANCER / Virgo

42. **DAY OF THE WEEK**
MONDAY, (What does Monday
mean to you?)

43. **DIRECTION OF ROTATION**
**MAN / CLOCKWISE**
**WOMEN / COUNTER**
Clockwise

44. **YIN and YANG ASPECT**
**MAN / YANG**
**WOMEN / YIN**

45. **ELECTRO-MAGNETIC POLARITY**
**MAN / POSITIVE**
**WOMAN / NEGATIVE**

46. **GEM STONE**
**Gem stones are selected according to color of chakra and ruling planet.**
PEARL, Hematite, Blood
Jasper, Garnet, Coral and
Ruby, Selenite, Beryl,
Moonstone, Yellow
Sapphire,

47. **AROMA THERAPY**
CEDAR, Clove

48. **HERBS**
ADDERS TONGUE,
Cabbage, Colewort,
Caltrops, Chickweed,
Clary, Cleavers Coralwort,
Cucumber, Cress, Daisy,
Dogtooth, Iris, Loose strife,
Ladysmock, Moonwart,
Pearlwart, Privet,
Pumpkin, , Purslain,
Saxifrage, Trefoil
Arrowhead

49. **ANIMAL CHARACTERISTICS**
**Behaves Like a/an:** ANT or an
Elephant

50. **LIFE CYCLE OF CHAKRAS IN**
MAN and WOMAN
SEVEN YEARS BY
SEVEN

**Chakra & individual year**

**Chakra and Seven Year Cycle**

**(1)** AGE 1 / 50
**(2)** AGE 8 / 57
**(3)** AGE 15 / 64
**(4)** AGE 22 / 71
**(5)** AGE 29 / 78
**(6)** AGE 36 / 85
**(7)** AGE 43 / 92

51. **Principle Nadi or Sen:**
Sumana, Ittha, Pingkala &
Nanthakrawat

52. **YOGA**
Hatha, Kundalini Yoga

# Korosot
# Second Chakra

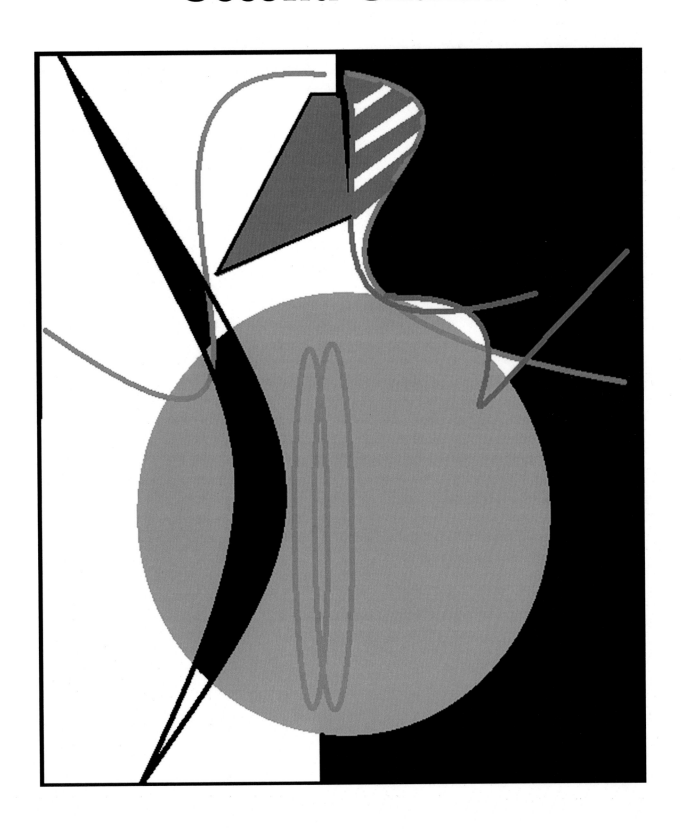

# Second Chakra:
# SVADHISTHANA CHAKRA
## ( Physical/ Emotional) (Purification )

Water is the source of all biologic life. We are conceived and nurtured for the first nine months of our life in water. Water is the natural environment of humans. Water is the first medicine and virtually all traditional healing mthods from very people of the world emphasize this at some point or another.

Three quaters of the earth is covered, or ruled, by water. Tides on the earth and in mankind are ruled by the moon. In the symbol or Yantra there is a circle and a crescent. The circle is water and the crescent is the moon.

Second chakra has the power reflecting these inner rhythms.

Second chakra relates on first chakra in the same fashion as the relationship of water to earth in    proportion. First chakra (Earth) supports, channels and underpins second chakra (Water).

The Yantra displays six petals for six sen. The petals also represent the six dimensions from which energy is received.

When thinking of the animal qualities of butterfly and crocodile, think of this. The qualities are serpentine, sensuous, tricky, deep diving, and able to float. There is such a thing as crocodile tears, a false display of emotions in order to manipulate, pretending and pretense, in order to consume or manipulate, perhaps sexually.

You see in the Yantra Vishnu: the deity of right living. In his hands he carries several symbolic objects, consider them:
1) **Conch** - The pure vibration or sound of liberation, the primordial OM.
2) **Chakra of light** - The Dhama, teachings of work or the way that we get in tune with timeless truth to gain life. Everything not in tune passes away.
3) **Club** - Metal of earth. The club is either a weapon or a buttress. This chakra controls the earth influence, but is dependent upon it for optimum function; security first, procreation second.
4) **Lotus** - The Lotus rising from the mud of earth, pale pink and luminous, pure and unaffected. The energy can become transcendent. Begin low and end high!

This chakra is the seat of Shakti, the most feminine aspect and God or Absolute in the creative aspect.

There is much inclination for play and playing!

Second chakra is erotic love, as compared to chakra #4 which is filial. This love is both pleasant and painful. Romance is based on eros, so emotions rule behavior and conscience and consciousness may be left behind. Hence the use of the skull symbol in some Yantra depiction's.

This is also the seat of the female impulse to create and to nurture new life.

This chakra is closely related to all processes of cleansing, purifying and detoxification. This center provides the impetus, or will and intelligence, for this process.

When open and balanced, there is an ease and attraction to the natural flow of life. You are open to others in a natural way.

As this chakra is the lower emotional center, it is fundamental in the process of first connection and physical attraction, which moves toward the expression of sex. There is nothing bad about this, it functions in much the same way as gravity, selecting and drawing us towards potential partners.

This is truly the center of gravity for our sex function and our capacity to express it positively, or not. It cannot be repressed healthfully as it's reasoning, energetically and vibrationally, is stronger and faster than the higher reasoning parts of us.This Definitely accounts for a world of interactions between all of us. We must acknowledge the sexual part of us and work through its manifestations to transform the energy into spirit food. This can only be done in the most loving and forgiving fashion. As attraction is spontaneous and to a degree impartial, all of us are equally subject to it. Let us claim our sexuality as an integral part of our being as humans and work out the healthy expression of it as a holy and sacred phenomenon just as any other integral part of us.

We must be sharp and use sharp tools to cut through the obstacles which hinder our awareness and development as whole beings.

There is duality of within and without. The center is where initial expansion and unfoldment of the  personality occur.

**Yoga:** The Yoga practice specifically for second chakra is Reishi Yoga, Tantra, Tai Chi and Chi-Gung.

**Proper Function:**  Acceptence of self and others. This chakra, the lower emotional chakra, gives us incentive, feeling and gusto for life. The caraving and movement to unite with and bond literally, physically with the world around us. To bond genuinely with the people around us. It's our reactions and feeling which are correct and true and represent a visceral consciousness and intuition. It brings us literally our gut reactions, positive or negative which guide us and keep us safe. Brings strength and vitality to the Astral body. It also enables us to remeber our astral journey.

**Balancing:** Moonlight, clear waters cleanse and stimulate, especially the full moon. Look in dreams around this time for insight into the activity of this center. Drink clean and pure water from as natural a source as you can find. Avoid bottled water if a fresh water source is available.

**Work:** Work heavily of the feet and the legs. Use big, broad and deep compression even to the point of bending the bones. Work indicated Sen and meridians. Release all key Wind GAtes, especially those in the legs. Do treatments and work points on the top of the head.

**Meditation:** By meditating on this center, the mind may reflect the earth as the moon does the sun. This brings creative and sustaining energy to life for art and for relationships, free of base desires which drag us into the mud. This is the first level of awareness other than earth, of other worlds.

# SVADHISHTHANA

Sanskrit: स्वाधिष्ठान

SACRAL CHAKRA

1. **SYMBOL**
**Second Chakra**

2. **COMMON NAME**
SPLEEN, Sex, Sacral

3. **SANSKRIT NAME**
SVADHISTHANA

4. **INTERPRETED MEANING**
DWELLING
place of the self

5. **FORM**
CIRCLE with CRESCENT

6. **TRADITIONAL SYMBOL**
6 Petaled Lotus Facing
down

7. **COLOR**
ORANGE

8. **LOCATION on the SURFACE of the body**
Over the Spleen

9. **LOCATION on the SPINE**
1st Lumbar Vertebrae

10. **PREDOMINATE SENSE**
TASTE

11. **SENSE ORGAN**
TONGUE

12. **WORK ORGAN**
GENITALIA

13. **ASSOCIATED GLANDS**
PARATHYROID

14. **FUNCTION of ASSOCIATED GLANDS**
Balances Calcium and
Phosphorus in Blood,
Controls Nerve Activity &
Utilization of Water
Metabolism

15. **SYMPATHETIC NERVE PLEXUS**
SPLENIC

16. **CHIEF SUBSIDIARY PARTS**
Gonad, Ovary &
Reproductive
System,Testis,Belly,
Sacrum, Lumbar
Vertebrae, Kidneys,
Bladder, Lymphatic Fluid,
Water, Semen, Saliva,
Mucus, Urine, Interstitial
Fluids

17. **MANTRA**
VAM, Bang, Bhang,
Mang, Yang, Rang, Lang,

18. **VOWEL SOUND**
" O", as in "November",in
the Key of D

19. **MUSIC THERAPY**
FLOWING,Sensuous,
Passionate, Playful,
Joyful, Fountains, Waves,
Running Water, La Valse (Ravel),
Symphanie Pathertique
(Tchaikovsky)

20. **EXAMPLES**
Venusberg Theme
(Wagner), Concerto a due
Chori (F1,No. 60, Vivaldi),
Acoustic Guitar,

21. **SUITABLE EFFECTS and/or INSTRUMENTS**
SITAR, Celtic Harp,
Classical Guitar, Violin,
Tambourine

22. **MUDRA**
One Palm Up/One Palm
Down

23. **ELEMENT**
WATER

24. **QUALITY OF THE ELEMENT**
PURITY

25. **BASIC BEING**
CREATIVE Reproduction
of Being

26. **ATTRIBUTE**
**Positive/ Negative**
PURITY & RECEPTIVENESS,
ATTACHMENT &
NON- EXISTENCE

27. **DESIRE**
SEXUALITY,
Gregariousness

28. **ACTIVITY**
FANTASY, Right
Livelihood, Procreation

29. **NATURE**
    COOL

30. **QUALITIES OF DESIGN**
    BRANCHING Forms,
    Flowing, Harmonious
    Lines, Arabesque,

31. **RESULT of Unsatisfied
    Karma, To be Reborn as:**
    ARTIST, Poet, Musician,
    Dancer, Designer,
    Architect

32. **LOKA, Plane of
    Existence**
    BHU VARA LOKA
    Astral

33. **VAYU, Type and Color of
    Vital Air**
    APANA / VYANA
    Orange / Red

34. **HINDU DEITY**
    VISHNU Lord of
    Preservation USHAS,
    LAKSHMI / Shakti

35. **GREEK DEITY**
    APHRODITE

36. **ROMAN DEITY**
    VENUS

37. **ETRUSCAN DEITY**
    TURAN

38. **BABYLONIAN DEITY**
    ISHTAR

39. **EGYPTIAN DEITY**
    HAT-HERUT
    (Hat-hor), Bast

40. **RULING PLANET
    Symbol**
    VENUS

41. **ASTROLOGICAL SIGN
    Symbol**
    LIBRA / Tarus

42. **DAY OF THE WEEK**
    FRIDAY

43. **DIRECTION OF
    ROTATION
    MAN /COUNTER**
    Clockwise
    **WOMEN /CLOCKWISE**

44. **YIN and YANG ASPECT
    MAN / YIN
    WOMEN / YANG**

45. **ELECTRO-
    MAGNETIC POLARITY
    MAN /NEGATIVE
    WOMAN /POSITIVE**

46. **GEM STONE
    Gem stones are selected
    according to color of
    chakra and ruling planet.**
    AZURITE, Coral, Blue
    Calcite, Emerald, Jade,
    Kunzite, Malachite,
    Peridot, Tourmaline,

47. **AROMA THERAPY**
    YLANG-YLANG,
    Sandlewood

48. **HERBS**
    ALKANET, Alehoof,
    Arrack, Artichoke, Beans,
    Bishopsweed, Burdock,
    Cherry, Cocks a head,
    Coltsfoot, Cowslip,
    Featherfew, Foxglove,
    Kidneywort, Mugwort,
    Peppermint, Ragwort,
    Sorrel, Thyme, Yarrow

49. **ANIMAL
    CHARACTERISTICS
    Behaves Like a/an:**
    BUTTERFLY & Crocodile

50. **LIFE CYCLE OF
    CHAKRAS IN**
    MAN and WOMAN
    SEVEN YEARS BY
    SEVEN

**Chakra &
individual year**

(1) AGE 2 / 51

**Chakra
and
Seven
Year
Cycle**

(2) AGE 9 /58
(3) AGE16 /65
(4) AGE23 /72
(5) AGE 30 /79
(6) AGE 37 /86
(7) AGE 44 /93

51. **Principle Nadi or Sen:**
    Khitchanna, Sumana,
    Ittha, Pingkhala, Kalatheri

52. **YOGA**
    Tantra , Kundalini Yoga,
    Chi-Gung

# Korosot
# Third Chakra

# Third Chakra: MANIPURA CHAKRA
### ( Physical/ Intellectual) (Ilumenation )

This Chakra gives us energy to live. Fire is light, warmth, energy, activity and purification. Contrast this with the purification qualities of water.

It is our power center, the Sun, in our system absorbing and distributing energy to feed our matrix or ethereal body, then vitalizing the physical.

This is the highest of the three lower, or eathly influenced, chakras.It is the intellectual, earthly, chakra.

Evidence of this chakra can be observed in a strong reactionary attitude in relating to others: we like them, we do not like them. Manipura is the foundation of our social personality, call this our FALSE personality.

It's principle duties are to purify and to bring up the energy of the lower, second chakra, controlling the creative energy and manifesting the energy of the higher chakra. This is what is meant by "Shapes our being". Under it's influence, one can separate useful from non-useful with the skill and dexterity of a surgeon scalpel.

Brings intelligence and consciousness to that of the physical body. Attitudes of opinion such as good or bad, friendly or unfriendly, pleasent or unpleasent etc.

Integrating our feelings increases inner light. Very strong in moods which reflect its open or shut status: Bright or Dark. The world is light or dark, it's inner light determines the clarity of the vision.

When this chakra is active one will react strongly in the physical as a forewarning of imminent, or potential, danger.

MANIPURA
Sanskrit: मणिपुर
SOLAR PLEXUS CHAKRA

**Key Concepts:**

City of Jewels, Shaping of being
Personality and False personality
Fire, light, warmth and vision
Integration of feelings
Intellect of the physical world
Independence
Positive attributes are Radiance and Perceptiveness
Negative attributes are Anger and Manipulation
Sight, Eyes, Liver and Stomach
Ulcers

**Yoga:** Jnana Yoga: The Yoga of Self realization and Karma Yoga, the yoga of selfless action. This brings our life into harmony with nature and divinity. ( See That Thou Art by Swami Vivekananda)

**Proper Function:** This chakra represents the lower intellectual chakra. Manifesting our light and life that we each bring into the world. Supporting a healthy and well adjusted expression of self and personality in relation to those around us. Strength of character couple with determined efforts sustained over time. The ability to see beyond the immediate events and the glaring distraction of immediacy with accurate perception. It bring the possibility of artful, dynamic and creative living. Life is not just tedious or challenging, it is exciting!

**Balancing Third Chakra:** Abandon any activity whose initial impetus was or is found in a negative emotion. This kind of activity is a self fulfilling negative prophesy which feeds and consumes itself.

To learn control, practice external consideration; simply think of others first. Cease expressing annoyance and show charity at every available opportunity, and if there is no opportunity, create one! Talk less. Learn and practice separating yourself from what happens to and around you. These occurances are events and you are not those events.

Diminish the expression of associative thoughts, first thoughts, opposite thoughts, likes and dislikes, as well as all purely subjective opinions. Increase your understanding. Compete less, compare less. Stop, or at least work on, not criticizing what you really do not understand.

Do not take small things too seriously.

When you are censured, don't justify.

Be benevolent, even to unjust persons.

Reproach neither others, nor yourself.

Choose to serve rather than to rule.

Don't push yourself to the front.

If you see someone in the negative expression of their third chakra - LET THEM BE! Do not fight or challenge.

Persuade without destruction or harm.
Avoid vengeful thinking, seek not to get back.

Pay the full price for something intentionally, even if you could "beat the price down".

Learn sincerity by not assuming that you know better.

Do not have hidden agendas. Make the inner as the outer and the outer as the inner.

Moonlight, clear water cleanses and stimulates, especially the full moon. Look in dreams around this time for insight from this center. Drink clean and pure water from as natural a source as possible.

**Disharmony:** Leads to inclination to manipulate, to control others, dominate. There is a lack of genuine sense of self worth. So self worth is sought out in others. The emotions tend to be stopped up. Look for floods and breakdowns. Easily upset, out of proportion to the apparent cause. Expressions of inadequacy, dejection, discouragement, obstacles which appear intentional, a lack of spontaneity, vigor and presence of uncertainty. Not feeling capable of dealing with the "Struggle for survival".

**Work:** Focus on immune system, lymphatic drainage, Detox for liver and colon. Breath work focused on the mid abdomen and diaphragm while working Sen Ittha and Pingkhala. Focus on Lom in hips and shoulders. Work light and relatively fast with less than deep pressure, except when releasing the wind gates. Include all abdominal focus such as 6 and 9 points and abdominal routine in general.

1. **SYMBOL**
   Third Chakra

2. **COMMON NAME**
   SOLAR PLEXUS , Navel

3. **SANSKRIT NAME**
   MANIPURA

4. **INTERPRETED MEANING**
   CITY of Jewels

5. **FORM**
   TRIANGLE

6. **TRADITIONAL SYMBOL**
   10 Petaled Lotus, Facing up

7. **COLOR**
   RED / GOLD

8. **LOCATION on the SURFACE of the body**
   Navel or Solar Plexus

9. **LOCATION on the SPINE**
   8th Thoracic vertebrae

10. **PREDOMINATE SENSE**
    SIGHT

11. **SENSE ORGAN**
    EYES

12. **WORK ORGAN**
    FEET and LEGS

13. **ASSOCIATED GLANDS**
    THYROID

14. **FUNCTION of ASSOCIATED GLANDS**
    Regulates Heat & Combustion of energy

15. **SYMPATHETIC NERVE PLEXUS**
    SOLAR PLEXUS

16. **CHIEF SUBSIDIARY PARTS**
    Upper lumbar Vertebrae, Stomach, Gall Bladder, Liver, Diaphragm, Digestive System, Small Intestine, Autonomic Nervous System

17. **MANTRA**
    RAM, Dang, Dhang, Rlang, Pang

18. **VOWEL SOUND**
    "O", as in "GOD", in the Key of E

19. **MUSIC THERAPY**
    WELL ORDERED, Graceful, Intellectual

20. **EXAMPLES**
    Canon in D major (Pachebel), Bolero (Ravel), Brandenberg concerto, no.6 (Bach)

21. **SUITABLE EFFECTS and/or INSTRUMENTS**
    XYLOPHONE
    Vibraphone, Electric Guitar, Tabla, Pan Pipes, Bell, Singing, Rushing Wind

22. **MUDRA**
    Pointing Finger

23. **ELEMENT**
    FIRE

24. **QUALITY OF THE ELEMENT**
    RADIANCE

25. **BASIC BEING**
    SHAPING of Being

26. **ATTRIBUTE**
    **Positive/ Negative**
    RADIANCE & PERCEPTIVENESS
    ANGER & MANIPULATION

27. **DESIRE**
    ACHIEVEMENT, Immortality, Authority, Name and Fame

28. **ACTIVITY**
    VISION, Hard Labor, Organization

**29. NATURE**
HOT

**30. QUALITIES OF DESIGN**
SEGMENTED Forms,
Counter charged patterns,
Mirrored Images,

**31. RESULT of Unsatisfied
Karma, To be Reborn as:**
KING, Royalty,
Administrator, Political
Leader, Elder, Chief

**32. LOKA, Plane of
Existence**
SVA LOKA Celestial

**33. VAYU, Type and Color of
Vital Air**
SAMANA / VYANA,
Solar Red

**34. HINDU DEITY**
BRADDHA RUDRA,
Power of Destruction,
GANESHA

**35. GREEK DEITY**
HERMES

**36. ROMAN DEITY**
MERCUROUS

**37. ETRUSCAN DEITY**
TURMS, Ciians

**38. BABYLONIAN DEITY**
NABU

**39. EGYPTIAN DEITY**
TAHUTI (Thoth), Sefekh
(Seshat)

**40. RULING PLANET
Symbol**
MERCURY

**41. ASTROLOGICAL SIGN
Symbol**
GEMINI / Virgo

**42. DAY OF THE WEEK**
WEDNESDAY

**43. DIRECTION OF
ROTATION
MAN /CLOCKWISE
WOMEN /COUNTER**
Clockwise

**44. YIN and YANG ASPECT
MAN / YANG
WOMEN / YIN**

**45. ELECTRO-
MAGNETIC POLARITY
MAN /POSITIVE
WOMAN /NEGATIVE**

**46. GEM STONE
Gem stones are selected
according to color of
chakra and ruling planet.**
AGATE, Aventurine,
Jasper, Mica, Pumice,
Citrine, Gold Peridot,
Tourmaline,

**47. AROMA THERAPY**
LAVENDER, Rosemary,
Bergamot

**48. HERBS**
GOLDENROD,
Amara dulis, Calamint,
Caraway, Wild Carrots,
Coraline, Cow Parsnip,
Dill, Endive, Fern, Fennel,
Germander, Haresfoot,
Hazelnut, Horehound,
Hounds Tongue,
Liquorice, Mandrake,
Marjoram, Mulberry,
Nailwort, Olive
Spurge, Valerian, Winter
Savory

**49. ANIMAL
CHARACTERISTICS
Behaves Like a/an:**
COBRA

**50. LIFE CYCLE OF
CHAKRAS IN**
MAN and WOMAN
SEVEN YEARS BY
SEVEN

### Chakra & individual year

| Chakra and Seven Year Cycle | |
| --- | --- |
| **(1)** | AGE 3 / 52 |
| **(2)** | AGE 10 / 59 |
| **(3)** | AGE 17 /66 |
| **(4)** | AGE 24 /73 |
| **(5)** | AGE 31 /80 |
| **(6)** | AGE 38 /87 |
| **(7)** | AGE 45 /94 |

**51. Principle Nadis or Sen:**
Pingkala, Sahatsarangsi
(Female), Thawari (Male)

**52. Yoga**
Jnana Yoga, Karma Yoga

# Korosot
# Fourth Chakra

# Fourth Chakra: ANAHATA CHAKRA
## ( Spiritual/ Emotional) (Transformation and Transition )

Anahata is the center of the whole system and connects the upper three chakra with the lower three. This is expressed in the Yantra, the two crossed triangles, one facing up and one facing down. It is mutable, allowing give and take. The element of air shows this mutability and ability to mold to any container. This is similar to the water quality of second chakra, but at a higher level of vibration.

It is through the activity of Anahata Chakra that we perceive beauty.

The fourth chakra changes images, pictures, words and sounds into feelings. It also changes   instinctive urges, sensations, and impulses toward compulsions into feeling with understanding. It's purpose is to achieve love. All inclinations for deep intimate contact, oneness, harmony and love, even when selfish, begin here. It is also the massage and bodywork chakra because of its association with the skin and extremities. It is also the origin of fear of separation.

When positively aspected, it releases unconditional love. When influenced by higher centers it is the manifestation of Bhakti or divine love of all creation, the purest essence o devotion.

It is the moving and movement centered chakra, the chakra of choices.

Supports insight into the joy or sorrow of others. Sometimes leading to duplicating or mimicing even physical pain.

It is this chakra that unites the functional relationship and integration of all of the Kosha or five bodies. The five Vedic bodies or Kosha are: Annamayi, Pranamayi, Manomayi, Vijnanmayai and Anandamayai or the Matter (physical), Prana (Vital Air), Mind (Intellectual), Knowledge (Awareness and being), Bliss (Spiritual) bodies.

Disharmony within it appears as stagnation, conditional love, inability to truly receive from others, vulnerability and dependence on others love, depression, sadness. As compensation, one may act in an impersonal manner, or all the way to being coldly indeferrent or even heartless and cruel.

**Yoga:** Bhakti Yoga, the Yoga of pure devotion, as well as, SomaVeda® Thai Yoga, the yoga of the practical expression of lovingkindness and Conscious Practical Adoration.

**Proper Function:** The ability to integrate higher and lower ideas and ways of being into a functional and practical life. This chakra, the higher emotional chakra, gives us the ability to know what is the meaning and experience of genuine love as well as the other so called unlimited states of mind such as compassion, joy and equinimity. It allows us to experience the possibility of transformation through combining and integrating knowledge and being. Allows us to communicate our emotional intelligence. Allows us to receive and manifest the guidance and information which originates outside of our self. Helps us to integrate influences of higher nature, art and consciousness as well as those higher influences and consciousnesses which we ourselves originate.

**Work:** Work hands and arms, chest and back in a band around the uper torso, skin to skin treatments with herbs and ils after general balancing, also treatments to cleanse, purify and detoxify the skin such as exfoliation's and scrub's, body shampoo's and water based treatments, wraps and aroma therapy applications, or all of the above as in the PanchaKarma protocol. Use music in session. Pranayama or focused and directed breathing is beneficial. Bring nurturing energy to the physical body. Focus on dispersing excesses in the male side and lines of the body.

**Meditation:** Great nature. Green country, spring time and flowers. Energy and qualities of the south. Chanting Mantra like the *Metta Sutra* (Heart Mantra) and *OM Namo*. Master the Metta Sutra and the concept of "generation of the Boddhichitta" Experience nature, bright sunlight, broad band light therapy, Sunflowers and ripe grains. Look in this bright center for the balanced development of personality, necessary to live in this world of mankind. Look for the opportunity to correct Karmic imbalance and generate merit and atone for errors through the grace of charity.

**ANAHATA**

Sanskrit: अनाहत

HEART CHAKRA

**1. SYMBOL**
Fourth Chakra

**2. COMMON NAME**
HEART

**3. SANSKRIT NAME**
ANAHATA

**4. INTERPRETED MEANING**
UNSTRICKEN

**5. FORM**
HEXAGRAM

**6. TRADITIONAL SYMBOL**
12 Petaled Lotus Facing down

**7. COLOR**
GREEN / PINK

**8. LOCATION on the SURFACE of the body**
Over the Heart

**9. LOCATION on the SPINE**
4th Thoracic vertebrae

**10. PREDOMINATE SENSE**
TOUCH

**11. SENSE ORGAN**
SKIN

**12. WORK ORGAN**
HANDS

**13. ASSOCIATED GLANDS**
PITUITARY
(Anterior)

**14. FUNCTION of ASSOCIATED GLANDS**
Directly stimulates Thyroid, Adrenals, Ovaries, Contributes to produce Sex Hormones

**15. SYMPATHETIC NERVE PLEXUS**
CARDIAC

**16. CHIEF SUBSIDIARY PARTS**
Heart, Pericardium, Lower lung, Chest, Breasts, Thoracic Vertebrae, Respiratory System, Skin

**17. MANTRA**
YAM, Kang, Khang, Gang, Yong, Jong, Tang

**18. VOWEL SOUND**
"AH", as in "Not", in the Key of F

**19. MUSIC THERAPY**
MAJESTIC, Uplifting, Romantic Harmonious, Sentimental

**20. EXAMPLES**
Air on a G string (Bach), Jupiter (The Planets, Holst), Selected (Aaron Copland)

**21. SUITABLE EFFECTS and/or INSTRUMENTS**
CELLO, Double Bass, Saxophone, Bass Drum, Hand Clap, Thunder storm

**22. MUDRA**
Open Hands

**23. ELEMENT**
AIR

**24. QUALITY OF THE ELEMENT**
CONTENTMENT

**25. BASIC BEING**
SELF ABANDONING of Being

**26. ATTRIBUTE**
**Positive/ Negative**
DEVOTION & GENEROSITY
RESTLESSNESS & VANITY

**27. DESIRE**
TO DO SOMETHING, Love, Devotion, Duty, Selfless Service, Compassion

**28. ACTIVITY**
MOVEMENT Attaining Balance Above and Below, Emotions

**29. NATURE**
INTENSE, Love

**30. QUALITIES OF DESIGN**
REGULAR Rhombic, &
Rectangular Forms,
Squares, Intersecting Lines,

**31. RESULT of Unsatisfied Karma, To be Reborn as:**
SAINTLY PERSON,
Devotee, Healer, Spiritual
Artist, Reformer, Medicine
Man or Women, Shaman,
Doctor, Therapist

**32. LOKA, Plane of Existence**
MAHA LOKA  Balance

**33. VAYU, Type and Color of Vital Air**
PRANA / VYANNA
Emerald Blue

**34. HINDU DEITY**
ISHANA RUDRA SHIVA,
Perpetual Happiness
INDRA

**35. GREEK DEITY**
ZEUS, Athena, Poseidon

**36. ROMAN DEITY**
JUPPITER,  Minerva

**37. ETRUSCAN DEITY**
TINIA,  Menrva, Nethum

**38. BABYLONIAN DEITY**
MARDUK, Adad

**39. EGYPTIAN DEITY**
HAPI,  Maat, Amun-Ra

**40. RULING PLANET Symbol**
JUPITER

**41. ASTROLOGICAL SIGN Symbol**
SAGITTARIUS / Pisces

**42. DAY OF THE WEEK**
THURSDAY

**43. DIRECTION OF ROTATION**
MAN / COUNTER
      Clockwise
**WOMEN** /CLOCKWISE

**44. YIN and YANG ASPECT**
**MAN** / YIN
**WOMEN** / YANG

**45. ELECTRO-MAGNETIC POLARITY**
**MAN** /NEGATIVE
**WOMAN** /POSITIVE

**46. GEM STONE**
**Gem stones are selected according to color of chakra and ruling planet.**
ROSE QUARTZ,
Lepidolite, Sugilite,
Emerald, Pink Sapphire

**47. AROMA THERAPY**
ATTAR of ROSE, balances and
tonifies

**48. HERBS**
ANIS SEED,
Bloodwort, Chervil,
Dandelion, Dock, Fig Tree,
Hearts tongue, Hyssop,
Liverwort, Myrrh, Thorn
Apple

**49. ANIMAL CHARACTERISTICS Behaves Like a/an:**
ANTELOPE

**50. LIFE CYCLE OF CHAKRAS IN**
MAN and WOMAN
SEVEN YEARS BY
SEVEN

### Chakra & individual year

| Chakra and Seven Year Cycle | |
|---|---|
| | (1) AGE 4 / 53 |
| | (2) AGE 11 /60 |
| | (3) AGE 18 /67 |
| | (4) AGE 25 /74 |
| | (5) AGE 32 /81 |
| | (6) AGE 39 /88 |
| | (7) AGE 46 /95 |

**51. Principle Nadis or Sen:**
Kalathari, Sumana, Ittha,
Pingkhala

**52. Yoga**
Bhakti Yoga

# Korosot
# Fifth Chakra

# Fifth Chakra: VISHUDDA CHAKRA
## ( Spiritual/ Physical) (Communication )

Vishudda chakra is the center of human capacity for expression and communication and all that this implies, including all of the different forms of human communication and art. It inspires the lightning of insight and inspiration.

It is really two chakras, there is a smaller branch that rises from the same base and opens to the back.

It is the bridge between our thoughts and feelings and our impulses and reactions. It is the vehicle of communication between all of the dispirit energies of the chakras and the world of humans. Every thing we know, sense, love or hate comes through here.

The elements earth, fire, water and air are made up of or formed from the element of ether associated with this chakra. Ether is the medium of sound, spoken word or divine word. Consequently creation was spoken into existence in many methodologies. Ether is Akasha, the astral place or plane of existence where all events, actions, thoughts and feelings that have occurred from the beginning of time are recorded. This is the beginning of the deepest insight; hearing the sound of creation.

It relates to non-verbal communication such as visual or performing arts, dance or music.

The development of this chakra creates space for the separation of higher mental functions from lower, so we become more objective. There is as an example, correlations of right or proper speech with correct mental functioning.

It has to do with our hearing; hearing the inner as well as the outer; such as hearing the voice of the spirit or spirit guides. It inspires our confidence in our knowing where we are going ourselves.

When harmonious, you express yourself, your feelings, thoughts and inner knowledge so that this is
reflected in the people and world around you. It is ok to reveal weakness because this is an attribute of inner honesty and humility.

When not repressed,  It's activity results in the fully expressed self. It enables one to listen, to listen well and wholeheartedly. It brings out the ability to speak with fully manifested intonation. It inspires the wisdom and confidence to say "No", when appropriate. Causing you to be free of  prejudice, It enables you to remain true to your inner voice of wisdom without being defensive. It results in the ability to communicate from other dimensions into this one.

Vishudda is the warrior chakra, it rules the way of the warrior. In extreme negative expression one may become violent as a result of pent up expressions and the resultant unresolved issues.

When not in harmony, it results in a restriction of communication between mind and body, causing a disconnection. Feelings are distant, difficult to express or thoughtlessly expressed. It may cause one to be shut off from the intellect. One may be very self critical,  utilizing this criticism as a filter for everything heard or said. It may result in concealing or hiding your inner being, so people do not know where they stand with you. You run away without warning and or attack in the same fashion. You are not able to express subtle distinctions of your thought processes. You are full of fear and judgmental thinking. One is reluctant to share knowledge which instead may bubble up in poems or anonymous contributions.

**Yoga:** The Yoga for fifth chakra is Mantra Yoga, Martial and Warrior Arts, Thai Nuad, PranaYama and Breath Work. Vipassana, Insight and walking meditation. Tai Chi Gung.

**Proper Function:** The higher physical chakra. Gives the power of hearing and speaking. Supports the developmental equation begun at first chakra in relation to security and survival. However, at a higher and more conscious level. When functioning properly actions in ife are appropriate and proportional to actual circumstances. There is resonance of expression of being evidenced by right actions, thoughts and deeds. One's "word" actually means something. The breathing and breath are full and unrestricted and the voice loud and clear. It supports the process of learning and acquiring new information life long.

**Work:** Work hands and arms, neck, chest and back in a band around the uper torso, Pranayama or focused and directed breathing is beneficial. Bring nurturing energy to the physical body. Focus on dispersing excesses in the male side and lines of the body.

**Meditation:** Recitation on Mantra, singing songs with finer and clarifying energy. Sacred chants and songs, Vipassana and walking meditation. Nuad performed as a dancing and or moving meditation with breath and internal focus.

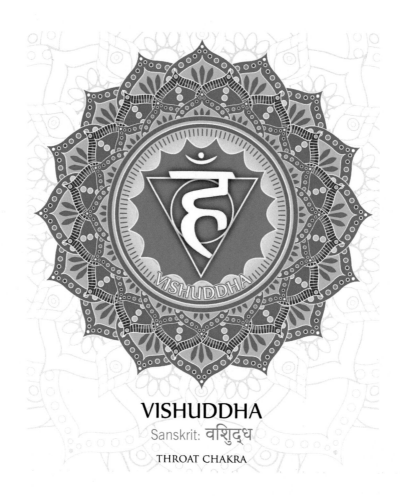

## VISHUDDHA
Sanskrit: वशिुद्ध

THROAT CHAKRA

1. **SYMBOL**
Fifth Chakra

2. **COMMON NAME**
THROAT

3. **SANSKRIT NAME**
VISHUDDA

4. **INTERPRETED MEANING**
PURE

5. **FORM**
CRESCENT

6. **TRADITIONAL SYMBOL**
16 Petaled Lotus Facing up

7. **COLOR**
BLUE

8. **LOCATION on the SURFACE of the body**
Lower Throat area

9. **LOCATION on the SPINE**
3rd Cervical vertebrae

10. **PREDOMINATE SENSE**
HEARING

11. **SENSE ORGAN**
EARS

12. **WORK ORGAN**
MOUTH  Vocal Cords

13. **ASSOCIATED GLANDS**
ADRENALS

14. **FUNCTION of ASSOCIATED GLANDS**
Affects Sodium & Potassium in Kidneys and Fats / Protein in Liver, Fight or Flight, Reproductive System,

15. **SYMPATHETIC NERVE PLEXUS**
PHARYNGEAL

16. **CHIEF SUBSIDIARY PARTS**
Throat, Arms & Hands, Mouth, Voice, Lungs & Brachial, Cervical Vertebrae, Neck, Trachea, Jaw

17. **MANTRA**
HAM. Ang, Ing, Ung, Ring, Lring, Aing, Ong, Aung, Ahang,

18. **VOWEL SOUND**
"EH" in the Key of G

19. **MUSIC THERAPY**
POWERFUL, Warlike, Assertive, Brash Orchestral,

20. **EXAMPLES**
Ride of the Valkyrie (Wagner), Mars (Holst), Fiery Rhythms...

21. **SUITABLE EFFECTS and/or INSTRUMENTS**
TRUMPET, Side Drum, Bagpipes, Whistle, Stamping feet, Sound of Fire, Volcano Erupting.

22. **MUDRA**
Pointing Up

23. **ELEMENT**
ETHER

24. **QUALITY OF THE ELEMENT**
UNITY

25. **BASIC BEING**
RESONANCE of Being

26. **ATTRIBUTE Positive/ Negative**
UNITY & ADVENTURE
EGO & DESTRUCTIVENESS

27. **DESIRE**
SOLITUDE, Knowledge, Wisdom

28. **ACTIVITY**
THOUGHTS and IDEAS, Expression, Communication, Knowledge

**29. NATURE**
VOID, Seeking

**30. QUALITIES OF DESIGN**
ZIG-ZAG and Pointed
Forms

**31. RESULT of Unsatisfied
Karma, To be Reborn as:**
TEACHER, Sage,
Interpreter of Scripture,
Guru, Khruu, Sifu,
Sensei, Scientist,

**32. LOKA, Plane of
Existence**
JANA LOKA, Human

**33. VAYU, Type and Color of
Vital Air**
UDANA / VYANA
Red / Violet

**34. HINDU DEITY**
PANCHAVAKTRA
Lord of Senses
AGNI / DURGA

**35. GREEK DEITY**
ARES, Hephaistos

**36. ROMAN DEITY**
MARS (Mavors), Volcanus

**37. ETRUSCAN DEITY**
MARIS, Sethlans

**38. BABYLONIAN DEITY**
NINURTA, Nusku

**39. EGYPTIAN DEITY**
HERU-BEHUTET (Horus
of Edfu). Sekhet (Sekhmet)

**40. RULING PLANET
Symbol**
MARS / Pluto

**41. ASTROLOGICAL SIGN
Symbol**
ARIES / Scorpio

**42. DAY OF THE WEEK**
TUESDAY

**43. DIRECTION OF
ROTATION**
**MAN** / CLOCKWISE
**WOMEN** / COUNTER
Clockwise

**44. YIN and YANG ASPECT**
**MAN** / YANG
**WOMEN** / YIN

**45. ELECTRO-
MAGNETIC POLARITY**
**MAN** / POSITIVE
**WOMAN** / NEGATIVE

**46. GEM STONE**
**Gem stones are selected
according to color of
chakra and ruling planet.**
RUBY, Turquoise Asbestos,
Flint, Red Garnet, Red
Jasper, Lava, Onyx, Blue
Sapphire Tourmaline

**47. AROMA THERAPY**
SAGE, Eucalyptus

**48. HERBS**
ALOES, Barberry, Basil,
Coriander, Garlic, Honey
Suckle, Horseradish,
Leeks, Mustard, Nettles,
Onions, Tobacco,
Wormwood,

**49. ANIMAL
CHARACTERISTICS
Behaves Like a/an:**
PEACOCK

**50. LIFE CYCLE OF
CHAKRAS IN**
MAN and WOMAN
SEVEN YEARS BY
SEVEN

### Chakra & individual year

| Chakra and Seven Year Cycle | Chakra and individual year |
|---|---|
| | (1) AGE 5 / 54 |
| | (2) AGE 12 / 61 |
| | (3) AGE 19 / 68 |
| | (4) AGE 26 / 75 |
| | (5) AGE 33 / 82 |
| | (6) AGE 40 / 89 |
| | (7) AGE 47 / 96 |

**51. Principle Nadis or Sen:**
Sumana, Ittha, Pingkala, Lawusang
(Female), Ulangka (Male), Kalathari

**52. YOGA**
Mantra Yoga, Martial and
Warrior Arts, Thai Nuad,
PranaYama and Breath Work.

# Korosot
# Sixth Chakra

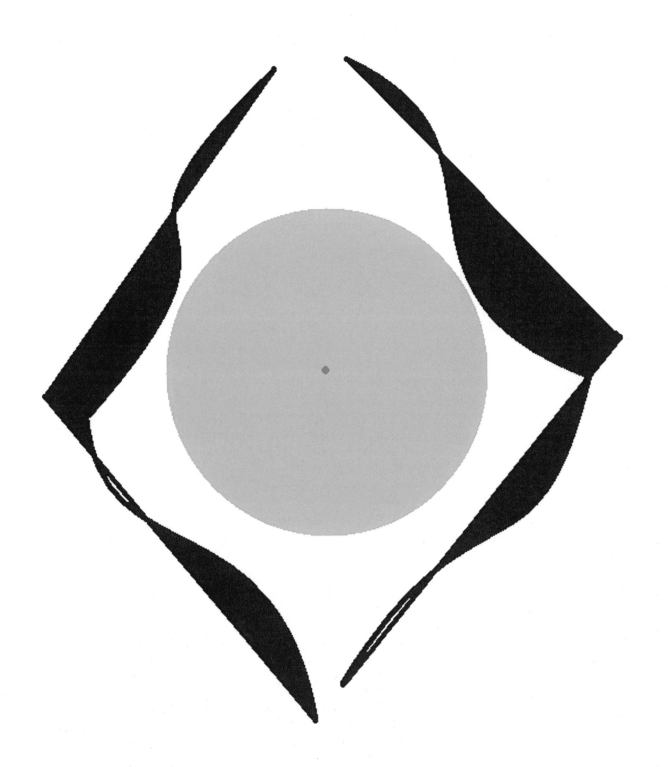

# Sixth Chakra: AJNA CHAKRA
## ( Spiritual/ Intellectual) (Intuition )

Through Ajna, one sees the herat of the matter. It reveals conscious perceptions of the true nature of being and is the seat of higher mental powers. It is the seat of will or discipline to do anything.

Physically there is a direct connection to the central nervous system.

There is a similarity to first chakra, in that it is the final repository of the three primary Sen, Sumana, Ittha and Pingkhala, although at their highest joining. It is the highest chakra on the body, ruling our life in this physical dimension.

Ajna is the seat of attainment of consciousness. It is the part of us bridging between the Absolute, the intelligence of the Sun, and the world of mankind. Ajna is the third eye, the abode of our sirit guide, our consciousness.

It allows us to create new physical realities superceding the old.

Ajna drives cellular metabolism, regeneration and healing. The heart may provide the initial inclination to move toward healing; however, it is this center which provides the intelligence, the know how, to actually do it.  When developed it drives the emotions, not the other way round. This energy is the manifestation of our imagination. It gives us access to perceptions beyond ordinary physical reality and it's inherent limitations. Ajna is the seat of Siddhi's (Special abilities) and ESP of all kinds.

When balanced with fourth chakra, it can direct and focus energy for healing externally. Few person's have an open sixth chakra, and if they did they might not let or want you to know.

It produces an active and creative mind. It inspires pursuit of questions for super normal knowledge and wisdom. It reveals a capacity for visualization. It's activity causes an openness to the mystic or esoteric side of life so we can get the sense of logic about the mysterious part of our life.

It enables more internally directed thinking, and thinking which leads to results in the material world. The material world becomes transparent.

It is the chakra of diplomacy.

**Disharmony;**  One becomes overly intellectual, analytical and organized. Think in terms of obsessive and compulsive behaviors such as: You are a bad authority figure. You are not wholistic. You permit yourself to be arrogant and prejudiced. You reject spirituality.

One indulges in the mental domination of others.

One might receive higher energy, but lack an understanding of it, perhaps with much distortion. Like a television set which almost but not quite receives the station you are trying to receive.

You may be forgetful and have poor vision.

You can lose your head, and since this is where you live, it can be especially traumatic.

It causes confused and muddy thinking.

One may be cold and distant.

**YOGA:** Jnana Yoga, the way of awareness based on developing the minds ability to distinguish between the real and the unreal, Vipassana. Yantra Yoga, using visual symbols to awaken, stimulate, and develop consciousness. Conscious art and Sacred Symbolism.

**Proper Function:** The higher intellectual chakra. Gives us sight and knowledge of the shape and nature of things. Acute perception of all natural things as well and the ability to actually see between realms of possibility and reality. Some say between worlds. Brings vision, understand, knowledge and realization and revelation. When unobstructe may bring so called ESP such as Clairvoyence. Perception of Aura's may be a 6th chakra function as well.

**Work:** Work the arms, wrist and upper chest neck, throat and jaw.

**Meditation:** Watch the starry deep blue night sky. Consider the infinity of celestial bodies drawing consciousness. Walk a labyrinth. Practice Vipassana Bhavanna meditation (Insight or Walking meditation).

# AJNA
Sanskrit: आज्ञा

THIRD-EYE CHAKRA

1. **SYMBOL**
Sixth Chakra

2. **COMMON NAME**
THIRD EYE , Brow

3. **SANSKRIT NAME**
AJNA

4. **INTERPRETED MEANING**
AUTHORITY Unlimited Power

5. **FORM**
CIRCLE with Two Petals

6. **TRADITIONAL SYMBOL**
96 Petaled Lotus
Facing (2x48) up

7. **COLOR**
VIOLET

8. **LOCATION on the SURFACE of the body**
Between the Eyes, Brow Ridge

9. **LOCATION on the SPINE**
1st Cervical vertebrae

10. **PREDOMINATE SENSE**
ALL SENSES,
Cognition & Intuition

11. **SENSE ORGAN**
ALL SENSE ORGANS

12. **WORK ORGAN**
WHOLE PERSON

13. **ASSOCIATED GLANDS**
PITUITARY (Posterior)

14. **FUNCTION of ASSOCIATED GLANDS**
Regulates Homeostasis of body, Balances energy of whole body.

15. **SYMPATHETIC NERVE PLEXUS**
CAROTID, Cavernous & Cephalic Ganglia

16. **CHIEF SUBSIDIARY PARTS**
Forehead, Ears, Nose, Left Eye, Base of skull, Medulla, Face, Sinuses, Cerebellum, Central nervous system

17. **MANTRA**
AUM Ksham

18. **VOWEL SOUND**
"E" as in "Easy" in the Key of A

19. **MUSIC THERAPY**
COSMIC, Brooding, Mystical, Transformative, Obscure, Celestial, New Age,

20. **EXAMPLES**
Finlandia (Sibelius), Pavane for a dead Infanta (Ravel), Saturn (HOLST),

21. **SUITABLE EFFECTS and/or INSTRUMENTS**
TAMBURA Deep Toned Gong, Bass Horns, Wood Blocks ,Strident Clangorous Sounds, Ocean Sounds

22. **MUDRA**
All Pointing Up

23. **ELEMENT**
MIND

24. **QUALITY OF THE ELEMENT**
BEING-NESS

25. **BASIC BEING**
KNOWLEDGE of Being

26. **ATTRIBUTE Positive/ Negative**
OPENNESS & OBJECTIVITY
DISTANCE & DOMINATION

27. **DESIRE**
CLARITY, Union, Unity, Realization,Intuition,Revelation

28. **ACTIVITY**
TRANSFORMATION, Transmutation

29. **NATURE**
NON-ATTACHMENT,
Knowing

30. **QUALITIES OF DESIGN**
ABSTRACT Designs based
on Natural Shapes,
Concentric Circles
suggesting Spatial
Perspectives

31. **RESULT of Unsatisfied Karma, To be Reborn as:**
ACETIC, Lama, Yogi,
Avatar, Buddha, Prophet,
Bodhisattva

32. **LOKA, Plane of Existence**
TAPAS LOKA
Austerity / Penance

33. **VAYU (Type and Color of Vital Air)**
PRANA / VYANNA
Emerald Blue

34. **HINDU DEITY**
ARDHANARISHVARA
(Shiva / Shakti),
Lord of Perfected
Consciousness

35. **GREEK DEITY**
HERA, Kronos, Aphrodite,
Ourania,

36. **ROMAN DEITY**
JUNO, Saeturnus

37. **ETRUSCAN DEITY**
UNI

38. **BABYLONIAN DEITY**
EA

39. **EGYPTIAN DEITY**
NET, Ptah

40. **RULING PLANET Symbol**
SATURN / Uranus

41. **ASTROLOGICAL SIGN Symbol**
CAPRICORN / Aquarius

42. **DAY OF THE WEEK**
SATURDAY

43. **DIRECTION OF ROTATION**
**MAN** / COUNTER
Clockwise
**WOMEN** / CLOCKWISE

44. **YIN and YANG ASPECT**
**MAN** / YIN
**WOMEN** / YANG

45. **ELECTRO-MAGNETIC POLARITY**
**MAN** / NEGATIVE
**WOMAN** / POSITIVE

46. **GEM STON**
**Gem stones are selected according to color of chakra and ruling planet.**
LAPIS LAZULI, Indigo Blue
Sapphire, Coal, Amethyst,
Alum, Amaronite, Hematite,
Obsidian

47. **AROMA THERAPY**
MINT, Jasmine

48. **HERBS**
AMARANTHUS,
Barley, Red Beet, Comfrey,
Flaxweed, Hemp, Horsetail,
Quince, Solomons Seal, Thistle

49. **ANIMAL CHARACTERISTICS**
**Behaves Like a/an:**
SWAN

50. **LIFE CYCLE OF CHAKRAS IN**
MAN and WOMAN
SEVEN YEARS BY
SEVEN

**Chakra & individual year**

| **Chakra and Seven Year Cycle** | (1) AGE 6 / 55 |
| | (2) AGE 13 / 62 |
| | (3) AGE 20 / 69 |
| | (4) AGE 27 / 76 |
| | (5) AGE 34 / 83 |
| | (6) AGE 41 / 90 |
| | (7) AGE 48 / 97 |

51. **Principle Nadis or Sen:**
Sumana, Ittha, Pingkhala

52. **YOGA**
Jnana Yoga, Yantra Yoga

# Korosot
# Seventh Chakra

# Seventh Chakra: SAHASRARA CHAKRA
## ( Spiritual/ Spiritual) ( Transmutation )

Sahasrara chakra is the seat of human perfection. It is the united energy of all of the other chakra. It is the true beginning and ending of the energetic cycle of the energetic or matrix body. It is where the personal energy field interfaces with the universe. It is the sphere of completeness, wholeness and integrity.

Sahasrara is where knowledge and being unite in total comprehension, beyond the vision or sphere of the third eye, as we no longer separate with arbitrary distinctions the real and the unreal. We see from the vaulted viewpoint of oneness with everything.

Any opening here is reflected s a raising of the vibrational level of all of the chakras.

The Seventh chakra cannot be blocked, only more or less open, more or less developed.

It is a call to slow down and look inside.

**Disharmony:** One is less open and will feel separate, apart or lonely and fearful. One may exhibit excessive external activity- sometimes called "Busy work". There may also be tangible and terminal illnesses common in this body.

**Yoga:** All forms of Yoga practiced at their highest level. Yantra Yoga, using visual symbols to awaken and stimulate.

**Proper Function:** The higher spiritual chakra. Perfects and compliments the attunement and communal or synergistic operation of all of the faculties. By faculties, I mean all of the functions of all of the other chakra. Seventh chakra, in representing information from the Atman, soul or spiritual guides and supports transformation and transmutation.

**Work:** Work off the physical body, on the light or matrix body.

**Meditation:** Alone on a high and or remote place, perhaps climbing close enough to touch the heavens. Classic fasting, Vision Quest or Sun Dance.

**SAHASRARA**
Sanskrit: सहस्रार
CROWN CHAKRA

1. **SYMBOL**
**Seventh Chakra**

2. **COMMON NAME**
CROWN

3. **SANSKRIT NAME**
SAHASRARA

4. **INTERPRETED MEANING**
THOUSAND petaled or
Place without support

5. **FORM**
CIRCLE as a Full Moon

6. **TRADITIONAL SYMBOL**
1000 Petaled Lotus

7. **COLOR**
WHITE / RAINBOW

8. **LOCATION on the SURFACE of the body**
Above the Crown of the
Head

9. **LOCATION on the SPINE**
Atlas / Axis

10. **PREDOMINATE SENSE**
SPEECH

11. **SENSE ORGAN**
E.S.P.

12. **WORK ORGAN**
SPIRIT

13. **ASSOCIATED GLANDS**
PINEAL, Thymus, Sex
Glands

14. **FUNCTION of ASSOCIATED GLANDS**
Higher Immune System
Function, Procreation, Psychic
Powers

15. **SYMPATHETIC NERVE PLEXUS**
CEREBRUM

16. **CHIEF SUBSIDIARY PARTS**
Cranium, Cerebral Cortex,
Right Eye

17. **MANTRA**
OM

18. **VOWEL SOUND**
"M" Hummed in the Key
of B

19. **MUSIC THERAPY**
SPIRITUAL,
Noble, Inspiring, Silence

20. **EXAMPLES**
Emperor Concerto
(Beethoven), The Ninth
Symphony (Beethoven),
Magic Fire Music
(Wagner), Selected
New Age

21. **SUITABLE EFFECTS and/or INSTRUMENTS**
FRENCH HORN
Tympani, Brazen Gong,
Crow Water Drum, Lyre

22. **MUDRA**
Closed Circuit

23. **ELEMENT**
SPIRIT

24. **QUALITY OF THE ELEMENT**
UNIVERSAL

25. **BASIC BEING**
PURITY of Being

26. **ATTRIBUTE**
**Positive/ Negative**
**There are only positive**
**attribues. There is no**
**Negative attribute.**

27. **DESIRE**
EXTENDED and perfect
ed consciousness, beyond
all categories or limita
tions perceivable, flowing
unobstructedly as the
pure and free manifesta
tion of energy and light.

28. **ACTIVITY**
TRANSFIGURATION

29. **NATURE**
SAMADHI, Panna, True Being

30. **QUALITIES OF DESIGN**
RADIAL Forms ,
Swirling Spirals

31. **RESULT of Unsatisfied Karma**, To be Reborn as:
NO longer subject to the turning of the wheel of KARMA, Life and Death, Birth and Rebirth. No bond with SUFFERING, Attaining NIRVANA when leaving the physical body. Infinity

32. **LOKA, Plane of Existence**
SATYAM LOKA
Truth / Reality

33. **VAYU, (Type and Color of Vital Air)**
VYANNA, Blue White

34. **HINDU DEITY**
THE GURU WITHIN

35. **GREEK DEITY**
APOLLO, Phoebus
Dionysus, Helios

36. **ROMAN DEITY**
SOL, Nomius

37. **ETRUSCAN DEITY**
CATHA, Hercle

38. **BABYLONIAN DEITY**
SHAMASH

39. **EGYPTIAN DEITY**
RA

40. **RULING PLANET Symbol**
SUN /Neptune

41. **ASTROLOGICAL SIGN Symbol**
LEO /Pisces

42. **DAY OF THE WEEK**
SUNDAY

43. **DIRECTION OF ROTATION**
**MAN** /CLOCKWISE
**WOMEN** /COUNTER
Clockwise

44. **YIN and YANG ASPECT**
**MAN** / YANG
**WOMEN** / YIN

45. **ELECTRO-MAGNETIC POLARITY**
**MAN** /POSITIVE
**WOMAN** /NEGATIVE

46. **GEM STONE**
Gem stones are selected according to color of chakra and ruling planet.
CLEAR Quartz Crystal,
Sulfur, Orange Calcite,
Diamond

47. **AROMA THERAPY**
LOTUS, Olibanum
Flat Cedar

48. **HERBS**
ALMOND,
Angelica, Ashtree,
Baytree, Camomile,
Celandine, Centaury,
Corn Hornwort,
Eyebright, Heart Trefoil,
Juniper, Marigold,
Mistletoe, Mustard, Olive,
Pimpernel, Rice, Saffron,
St. Johns Wort,
St. Peters Wort, Sundew,
Walnut,

49. **ANIMAL CHARACTERISTICS**
**Behaves Like a/an:**
PURE ILLUMINATION

50. **LIFE CYCLE OF CHAKRAS IN**
MAN and WOMAN
SEVEN YEARS BY
SEVEN

**Chakra & individual year**

**Chakra and Seven Year Cycle**

(1) AGE 7 / 56
(2) AGE 14 /63
(3) AGE 21 /70
(4) AGE 28 /77
(5) AGE 35 /84
(6) AGE 42 /91
(7) AGE 49 /98

51. **Principle Nadis or Sen:**
Sumana, Ittha, Pingkala

52. **YOGA:**
All forms of Yoga practiced at their highest level. Native American : Sundance, Vision Quest, Sweat Lodge or fasting.

# What does the theory of Chakra teach us?

The Chakra system is both a literal and a metaphorical model. It illuminates both the inner flow of energy and the transmutation and transformation of energy between the worlds we exist in, inner and outer.

We are the first Chakra, literally a bridge between heaven and earth.

The Chakra system illuminates how we are part of a greater cosmos and world. It gives us a working model for how the influences and energies of the greater world manifest within us and how we relate to that same greater world. This follows the "As above, So Below maximum. This As above , So below is demonstrated in the planetary correlations with specific Chakra on the one hand and the organic, physical correlations on the other. In other systems such as in Traditional Chinese Medicine and Taoism this relationship is illustrated in the concept Macro and Microcosms.

It shows how our mechanical bodies, anatomy and physiology relate to one another from an energetic and functional point of view.

It shows how we relate to the kingdoms of animals, vegetables and the mineral world.

It shows how we relate to the living air and water of our planet.

It gives us a model for the energy composition, circulation and flow within us. It shows literally how Prana, Chi, Orgonne, Energy, Ki, Vital Life Force or the Breath etc. move within us and the method of that movement. This is demonstrated by the heirachy of Chakra: the seven primary Chakra, the 108 seconday Chakra called Marma or Lom, the 621 tertiary Knots, Granthis, Muladra and the eighty eight thousand "all that there is" infinite points where literally every cell recives and communicates life.

It shows us the How and the Why of energy circulation from our core to our extremeties via Prana Nadi, Sen Lines and Meridians. Chakra are the pumps and valves orchestrating the flow of Prana to every part of every part.

It gives insight into how the five bodies, sheaths or Vedic Kosha of Annamayi (Matter), Pranamayi Vital Air), Manomayi (Mind), Vijnanmayi (Knowledge) and Anandamayi (Bliss) manifest and interact within us and in our daily lives.

The Chakra system demonstrates the complexity of our inner life of mind, feeling and emotion. It shows both the strenghts, weaknesses as well as the positive and negative attributes we all share.

It teaches us that all thought we may have at one time or another a dominance of one Chakra versus another that this dominance and manifestation is cyclical and that eventually we will cycle through the influence of all of the Chakra. This lesson among other things shows us how similar we all are in so many ways. The only real differences between us is where are we on the wheel of influence and manifestation.

Chakra have polarity. Their positive or negative attributes both illustrates the duality in our nature of the masculine and feminine but that these two seemingly opposites must be in balance for us to enjoy a harmonious and happy, healthy existence.

The Chakra provide us with a logical model, a road map 9for self development and conscious enlightenment.

The Chakra can give us insight into who and what we really are. Vessals of communication and expression of life force and energy, consciousness and materiality, co-sharing  and co-facilitating as partners of the co-creation of the universe.

# Korosot Chakra Body Types

## The psychology of Chakras in human development and classification of Chakra Korosot body types.

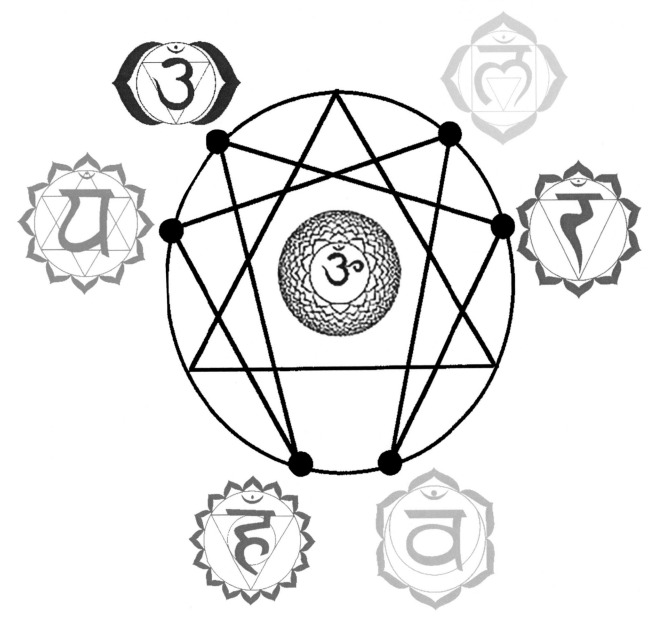

**Gurdjieff Enneagram Diagram with Seven Chakra Yantra or Symbols**

## Recognizing Korosot based Chakra Body Types

The theory of the chakras or energy vortices of light within is hardly a new age idea. This theory dwells in the ancient history of mankind, taking possibly a greater precedence in past times. It belongs to past ages of man when perhaps there was a greater and more sophisticated psychological understanding. Chakras are vortices of light, and clues to the inner development of man. They are maps of our entire being and doorways to the inner self. They are centers of information about the roles that we play in the external world as coexisting human creations.

Chakra is a Sanskrit word, it is common to the east Indian, Hindu or Thai teachings, Although popularly referenced to in the East Indian traditional scriptures, the theory of energy vortices or wheels of light within man and their correspondences is not the exclusive intellectual property of the Hindu traditions. Neither is the idea of chakra body types exclusively theirs alone.

Each type has various traits peculiar to it and distinctive to it as well. There are also some shared qualities. Qualities that illustrate the idea of harmony and relationship a;nonage or between each of the chadors and chakra types that are reflections of them.

First of all there is only one body, one mind, one self, one spirit, a luminous being of which our tangible physical body is only the nits gross and external manifestation. We are luminous beings and are unable to know or to see this in the ordinary way that we have of looking at our selves. The real sleighs not visible to ordinary persons in their common state. The real self is a reflection of the absolute according to the principle of scale. The ancient Alchemist Hermes Trismegistus stated this principle succinctly; AS ABOVE SO BELOW. We as human beings are a microcosm of the universe in which we live, part and participle of all organic life.

Our multi-dimensionality bridges a gap between the heavens and the earth, transmuting and transforming these energies from above and below. We are the vehicle through which the earth sees the stars and through which the stars feel the wet grass sliding between their toes. Our solar system is the most immediate universe that may reflect something of ourselves. To a lesser degree we reflect and manifest within, a particular ray of creation or octave that descends directly from the infinite origins of all creation to our own solar system.

This branch or Ray of Creation then descends further until it is evidenced within our very being. Inquiry has shown a me understanding of these principles exists in many traditions both eastern and west. I am referring here to the Esoteric, Hermetic, Stoic, Alchemical and Metaphysical inner sanctum of traditions; from India to Egypt, from Turkey to Ireland, including the North American continent as well. CHAKRAS and their correspondences, as well as the types of men associated with their principle influences, all together provide us with a way of learning and exploring not just OUR SELVES but the world we live in. We see in them the world of the EARTH, and our world's world, the SOLAR SYSTEM of our SUN in the spiral arm of the MILKY WAY. Chakra type is a reference framework to enable us to see attitudes and inclinations, strengths and weaknesses, attractions and repulsion's rising out of our basic nature. In fact, this system is a unique way of describing what our basic nature is really like . Chakras are not just things but who's.

Theoretically, there are seven types of persons that reveal the interplay of our own internal energy in a palpable way. There are seven different types of human beings which reveal the interplay of celestial based influences within each of us. The various influences become palpable in the play of life between all of these types. The rhythm and discourse, harmony and discord between each of the principle chakras and chakra derived types eventually becomes visible and tangible as the personality, character, emotions, intellectual propensities, attitudes and especially all of the purely mechanical actions of people. What we like most and dislike the most equally reveal our personality and the development of our individual character. Our core, our real essence or personality is the manifestation of chakra energy being deployed through the filter of our individual lives in the natural world. The state of our inner development and balance reflects the outer as well. We are a permeable membrane with powerful influence on both sides. The existence of chakras and their rules of behavior are found in the realm of non local phenomena. We actually cannot define the limitations of their influence and relativeness to all things known and unknown. There are many different manifestations of chakric energy.

Each chakra contains within it the latent influence of all of the other chakras. When we are refining to a Type (Chakra Body Type), we are making a statement about the observable, dominate or active influence. For example, when I refer to a# 2 Type, or to a second chakra body-type, what I am referring to, is a type of person where the influences of the second chakra are relatively more observable, dominant, or active, though not necessarily exclusive. Usually what we see in any given Type is where the individual is primarily reflecting or demonstrating the activity of the active principle chakra and to a slightly lesser degree the latent influence of two other chakras secondarily. All of the remaining chakras are there exerting their influence, however, to a still lesser degree.

We know what the latent secondary influence is. This influence being, according to the progression of light or energy within the chakra system, the chakra ahead and the chakra behind. In the case of our particular example, that of a second chakra type, the chakras would be chakra # 1 and Chakra # 3 respectively. After noting the latent secondary influences of Chakras # 1 and # 3 we then may account for the influences of the remaining latent chakras . In other words, we see not only where a person is presently seated, but at the same time where they have come from and the possibilities for their progress.

There is no such thing as a pure type. We all share all of the attributes and characteristics of every type in some way or at some point in our own evolution and life. Chakra types is a clue an insight or snap shot into where your at at a particular point or moment in time. Non of the types are better or more favorable than another. They all have and share strengths and weaknesses.

### Some of the roles that the various types play out in society.

| | |
|---|---|
| Korosot First Chakra Type | Contributes work and eccentricity |
| Korosot Second Chakra Type | Contributes growth, breeding and care |
| Korosot Third Chakra Type | A conduit for personality, intellect and crime |
| Korosot Fourth Chakra Type | Teaches, amuses, heals, and binds society together |
| Korosot Fifth Chakra Type | Wages war, Contributes communication, guards the realm, and pioneers new territory |
| Korosot Sixth Chakra Type | Stabilizes the whole and governs it |
| Korosot Seventh Chakra Type | Brings charisma and sparkle to all |

All types are necessary in the world as they are all necessary within ourselves. Types refer to the essence of us, the real core of us. There are so many questions that the theory of chakra types bring to the mind. What are their distinctive characteristics? Why are some types more or less compatible with one another? What is the apparent inclination of some to stay the same , and the tireless preoccupation of others to change all about? Why is it that some types can only be seen or clearly delineated with the help of a second or a third? Do they have distinctive personalities, psychology's and physical profiles? And if they do what are they and what do they look like?

The more we look at the question of types the greater the number and complexity of the questions that we are forced to consider. What I would like to do here is to present the theory of chakra body types in such a way as to answer many of these questions as feasible. On another level I would like to create in you' mind some questions and considerations not previously addressed. The science of chakra studies is a veritable encyclopedia of information about every conceivable aspect of human development. The organization inherent within the relationships between the chakras tells us much about the organization between you and I. Additionally there is much information within the system to enlighten us about our roles and responsibilities in the lawful order of the universe. It was never a truer statement made than t, let him with eyes to see, see, and him with ears to hear, hear.

One of the first and most important lessons to come out of the theory of chakras is that man is a COSMOS. What is a cosmos in my definition? A cosmos is a complete creation, made in the likeness or in the model of a universal model. It contains within itself all possibilities including but not limited to those of self consciousness and self transformation. A cosmos must contain at least three parts, each of which receives and processes a different kind of food or sustenance from without. There are six functions which digest, transform, utilize and combine these three foods, creating from them all the energy, matter and understanding of which the cosmos is capable. The six functions and the three foods together give rise to many different processes which develop according to the law of musical octaves; the functions standing for the full notes and the foods entering at the recognized half tones.

For a more thorough explanation of this teaching of G.I. Gurdjieff, see Rodney Collins book, The Theory of Celestial Influence. There is an outer circulation of chakra energy commonly depicted. This is the fairly common representation of the chakras on a line beginning at the bottom of the body and progressing to the crown of the head. A straightforward picture, but not entirely an accurate one. The same authors who will declaratively state that the chakras are energetic centers of influence will try to pinpoint them exactly on a physical body. This practice does not seem ,to me,to be a logical one, nor is it strictly speaking a traditional one. It seems to make much more sense to

Ancient Thai Codex give insight into the spiritual basis for Thai Ayurveda and related healing arts.

consider that an energy center within our physical body would in fact tend to have a sphere or field of influence.

And if there are to be many of these so called energy centers within the confines of our bodies then there would exist complex and overlapping fields of influence.

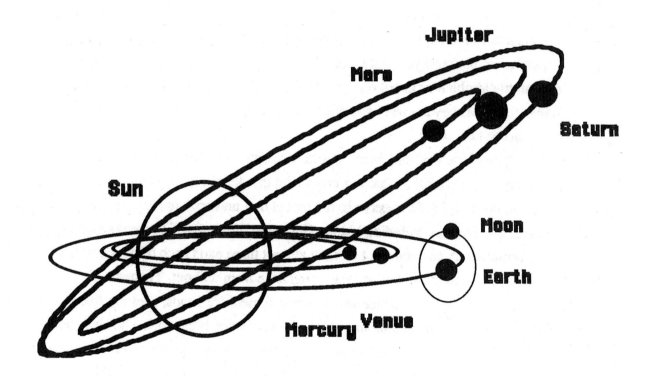

## The Solar Perspective

This new picture begins to look more like a person as we might encounter them, complex with many overlapping aspects.

I refer again to the idea of cosmos. It is now commonly known to the scientists who study the science of space, our solar system _and the larger picture of the universe, that there is no void in space. Every part of space is filled with matter and energy. Every square centimeter of our solar system feels the pull and radiation of the sun for instance.

The gravity's and magnetic fields of each of the planets around the sun affect each other and overlap and produce various harmonics between them in space. And if within man, man himself is a microcosm of the celestial beings and energies which have spawned him, then he will have a similar makeup. Just as the various members of our solar system do not confine the expression of their beingness to their particular geography or local in space, and reach out to affect and interact with all of the other members.

Our chakras within us are not confined to any anatomic location . They rather tend to have fields of influence, being of more or less radiant proportional to the inverse of the distance from a particular chakra to any of the others.

In particular by looking at the flow or circulation of light within the confines of the solar system, of the planets which especially rule or influence the chakras we can see integral organization between the chakras themselves. We can then see the next higher octave of developmental expression of chakra energy in the world of men CHAKRA BODY TYPES.

In the solar system visible to us, we establish that there is a circulation of light or scale of a discernible brilliance of light. The sun is the absolute brightest and beginning point of this scale. Reflecting the suns light, but with diminishing radiance, we see the Moon, Venus ,and Mercury within the elliptic of the earth's orbit. We then see the suns light reflected with increasing brilliance in Saturn, Mars and Jupiter outside of the plane of the earth's elliptical orbit. This then gives to us a precise order of circulation i.e. Moon, Venus, Mercury, Saturn, Mars and Jupiter. (See Chart Page 72)

We then apply this pattern or order of circulation of celestial light to the cosmos of Chakras in man. By relating the celestial cosmos of our solar system to the cosmos within man we see the chakras as a reflection and restatement of the universal circulation of light. We begin to come to the practical understanding of not only our nature as luminous beings but of the variegated and diversely tuned manifestations of universal light that we find ourselves to be. (See Chart Page 74)

Each and every one of us is subject to this order and progression of the light and the vibrations of heaven. All of mans inclinations and potentialities as humans find their fundamental origin here. The circulation of light energy within us in this order, and the harmonics it creates, bonds people. Throughout history, the present now, and infinitely into the future, the progression and movement of the stars within our solar system has... (Cont. Page 77)

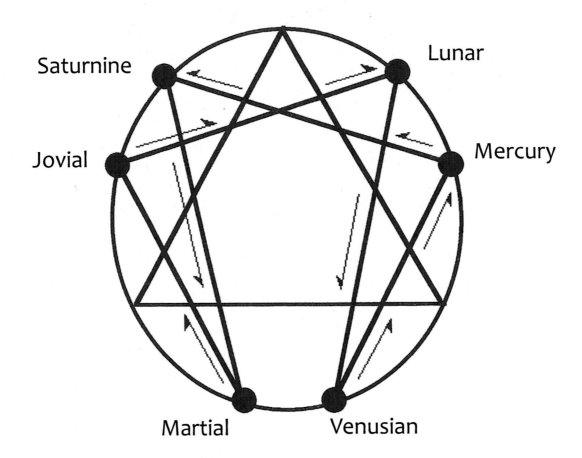

## Gurdjieff Enneagram

### Planet Correlation & Circulation of Light

**Chart No. Three**

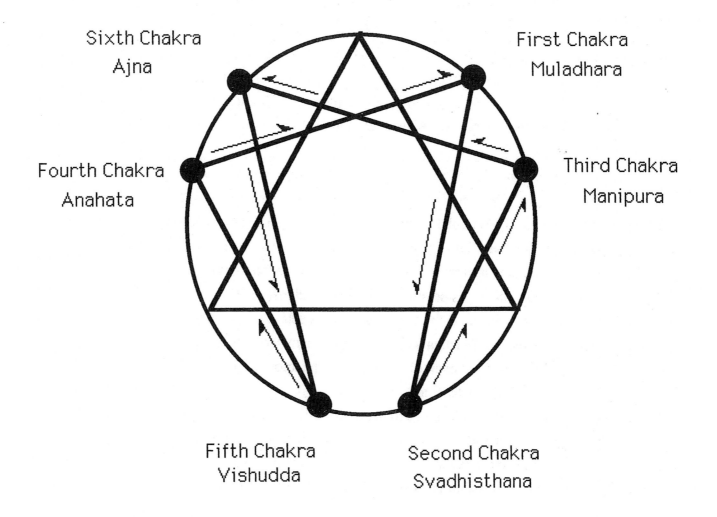

# Chakra Correlation & Circulation of Light

**Chart No. Four**

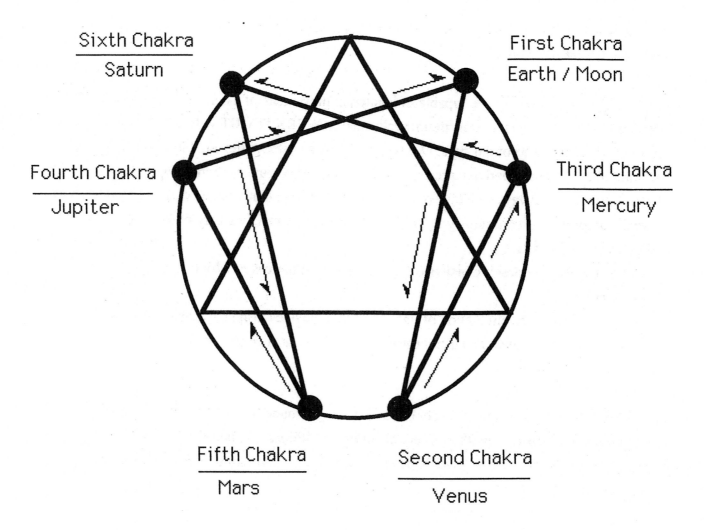

Sixth Chakra
Saturn

First Chakra
Earth / Moon

Fourth Chakra
Jupiter

Third Chakra
Mercury

Fifth Chakra
Mars

Second Chakra
Venus

# Chakra Correlation & Corresponding Planet

**Chart No. Five**

and will continue to shape, mold, constrain, and inspire us.

The beginning of wisdom is the knowledge of the self.

An impartial witness objectively describing essential inclinations, attitudes, characteristics, strengths and weaknesses is invaluable in the pursuit of knowledge. The knowledge of chakra types is a foundation teaching, a liberating teaching.

The clear sight provided allows us to begin the hard work of freeing ourselves from the pretense, imitation and imaginations that might be held about ourselves. By seeing what we are in the most elemental and mechanical fashion, we gain valuable insights and clues into our possibilities. One of the liberating ideas following ,is that the concept of the circulation and progression of energy provides us with the notion of our own progression and movement.

We can move beyond the level of current constraints and limitations. The universe is clearly with us on this one, having set the most glorious and perfect precedents above us. ( See Chart Page 75)

The movement we are capable of is internal movement of a conscious nature. We are within the context of our lifetime relegated to WORK IT OUT with the external features and limitations of our type. Our type which demonstrates the combined heritage of familial and celestial heritage present from the moment of our conception to our birth. Externally we will always be inclined to be short, tall, round, thin, light or dark, however, internally, spiritually, consciousness is a different matter. Internally we may make much progress as individuals.

*All work on oneself consists in choosing the influences to which you want to be subject.*

The order of the circulation of light within us provides insight and answers to the questions that efforts toward conscious development must generate. (See Chart Page 75)

No chakra type is qualitatively better or more profound in its role and function in the symphony of life than another. Every chakra type fulfills a role better suited or filled by no other. In the movement towards perfection all of the chakras must be in harmony for a change in level to occur.

The next higher type or progression of development is personal to you. All types have their false or negative psychological attributes which they struggle with and all have the same opportunities . Growth, transformation or depreciation and stagnation, are equally available to each.

**All of the chakras are active in every type. There is virtually no such thing as a pure type.**

If there was such a thing as a pure type, they would be virtually impossible to discern, or to read as they would be balanced with few distinguishable traits. The more balanced between all of the chakras the more difficult they would be to read. These examples of theoretical Chakra types are by nature of design unreal as they suggest the predominance of one specific chakra. Instead, what we see is a blending or types to varying percentages and levels of activity following the order of their natural progression., changing all the time.

When generally speaking of types we then would refer to them as follows; #1, #1, 2, #2, #2-3, #3, #3-4, #4, #4-5, #5, #5-6, #6. The number seven chakra body type is not listed here as a separate type as the number seven type is actually a potential amalgamation of any of the individual types. The seven is always seen as a 1/7 or a 2/7 or any other combination for example.

An even better way is to use a triad of the chakras which not only shows the dominate and progressive inclinations but illustrates the history of the type as well. In this case we see: #4-1-2. This shows the number one of a first chakra type moving from the bright #4 toward the feminine and passive energy of a #2.

I would expect this type of individual to principally exhibit the traits of a number one, with the additional traits of fourth and second to a lesser degree. Movement toward the fourth chakra traits would appear as history or retrograde and movement toward the second chakra traits would be possible progressive. The rest of the profiles would appear as follows: #1-**2**-3, #2-**3**-6, #3-**6**-5, #6-**5**-4, #5-**4**-1.

Now, the triad relationship of the active, passive and reconciling force of each type is presented. In this schemata the #7 Ctype is not referred to as separate as it is considered to be a potential modifier of a particular type. So a seven type would be referred to as a seven in a #2 for example. Additionally, it is notable that as we progress around the circuit of types completing a circuit from #1 to #4, and as the #4 type moves to #1 via the influence of #7 , we do not return to the same #1 type that we left before.

The next transition to #1 represents a new level of energy; a new octave of higher development possibly due to the extraordinary influence of the planet Neptune.

Knowledge of the chakra types can help us to understand and accept ourselves and others as they are. It is possible to operate out of a position of understanding why those around us are the way that they are. It is possible to understand why we and they

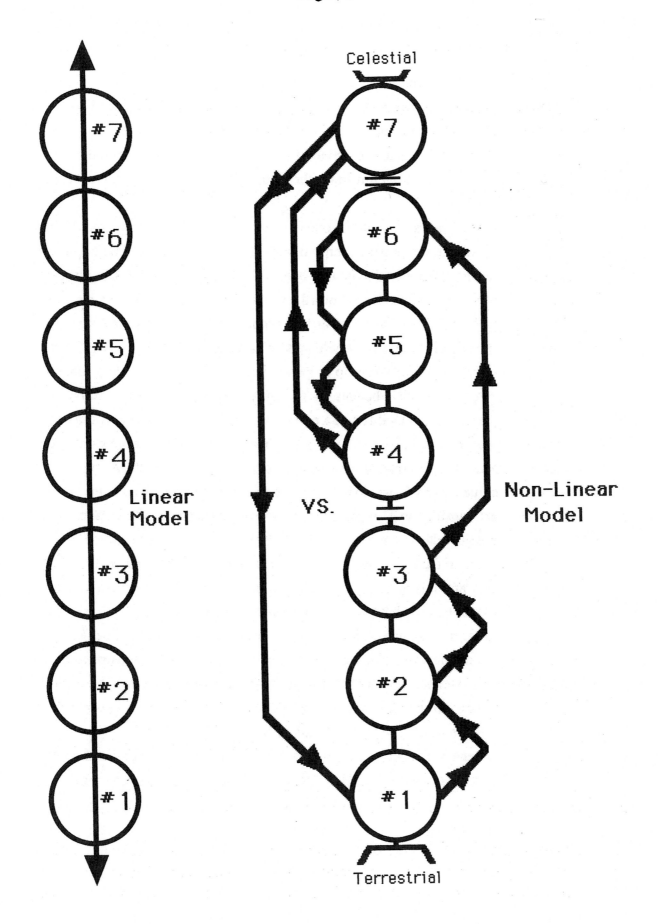

Linear
Model

VS.

Non-Linear
Model

Celestial

Terrestrial

react to each other in the many ways that we do. The natural attractions and repulsion's are made clear. By consciously moving ourselves forward on the line of development demonstrated by the chakras, we can consciously select the influence that we wish to be under. We can choose to move away from and abandon those less productive energies facilitating our own development.

We are now willfully participating in the cosmic dance.

This awareness may prevent us from becoming improperly crystallized, fixed or stuck in the influence of one center. ***Moving forward on the chart we lose nothing and gain everything.*** (See Chart Page 79)

The Linear vs. the Non-Linear models show some obvious differences. In the linear model, the one most people will be familiar with, the progression of energy is regular and progresses in even steps from the ground to the crown. Each Chakra in turn overlaps the influence of the preceding and the proceeding. The idea is that all of the Chakra are active all of the time. There is some consideration given that one or another Chakra might be more active than another. There is however, no conventional model as to why these changes might occur nor as to whether or not these changes might also have a cyclical pattern.

We use this model as our model for the external cycles and progressions of the Chakra influences. By external, I am mostly referring to our life in the greater world. For the internal life we look to the Non-Linear Chart based on the Enneagram. From a developmental point of view it is quite different. Immediately apparent you would first see the order of circulation is not so straight forward as progressing from bottom to top!

Next you notice there are gaps! Meditate on these gaps. Once you see them they make perfect sense. If the lower three Chakra are about the physical influences and energies and three upper are about the heavenly or spiritual, then how does one energy or influence become the other and vise versa? That puts a gap between #3 and #4. The gaps suggest either "you can't get there from here" or that you have to go a different direction to bridge the gap.

The next gap is between #6 and #7. This is interesting indeed. Conventional Chakra theory says that Ajna Chakra opens the door to enlightenment (Linear Model), however, the Non-linear model suggest either you can't get there from here or there must be another direction to come from to fill the void or bridge the gap here as well.

Actually what the chart show clearly is that the pathway towards realizing the influences of the seventh Chakra is via #4 or the heart!

Keep in mind as we have and share the characteristics of all of the Chakra, there is no such thing as a pure type.

# The Korosot First Chakra Type

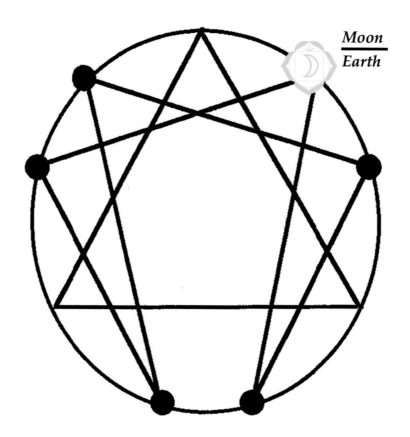

*Moon*
---
*Earth*

# KOROSOT FIRST CHAKRA TYPE

## The EARTH/ MOON CENTERED TYPE

ARTEMIS

## SANSKRIT NAME

The chakra name- MULADHARA, which means root or foundation.

## PLANETARY INFLUENCE

This chakra type is ruled by the Earth and the Moon and is clearly Lunar.

## ELEMENTAL INFLUENCE

The prominent element observable in this type is Earth. This contributes substantially to their distinct physical attributes.

## POLARITY & ACTIVITY

A negative, passive, female type. The mid-most feminine type. They like to collect and save things.

## GREEK& ROMAN ARCHETYPE

The Greek and Roman archetypes for this Ctype are Artemis and Diana

## PHYSICAL DESCRIPTION

Look for round face and a general roundness in features. Their is an inclination to retain water. Limped is a word that comes to mind. Men appear soft, vulnerable, and feminine superficially, but may be quite solid underneath. They prefer to blend with the prevailing environment or surroundings, even to the point of appearing camouflaged. They will tend to wear darker colors, and prefer black. The first chakras closet is full of the same muted colors. Their sense of fashion and ensemble runs to the opposite of the spectrum of flamboyance seen in the colorful Fourth chakra type. When not wearing black they will wear mismatched colors in off beat combinations. They are never quite with it from a fashionable point of view.

Their inclinations toward any movement are slow and periodic. First chakra types have been in the past depicted as classically beautiful. They may be very feminine, soft, curvy, delicate and light complected skin. Generally though in life we find their bodies oddly childish or not fully finished in appearance. Sometimes they might appear lumpy or strangely proportioned appearing older than they really are. In personal habits there may be on the one hand a complete disregard for hygiene or a compulsive fastidiousness, perhaps as a form of compensation.

They do not need a lot of sunlight to be happy and may often be inclined to spend many hours in small, tight or dark environments.

In yoga and ayurveda, First Chakra types are ascribed the animal characteristics of the ANT and the ELEPHANT. Also there is an inclination toward nocturnal activity reminds me of owls, rabbits or even creatures which live in the ground such as voles or moles and the like. We must take care of ourselves physically, staying reasonably fit. We must rehabilitate any and all injuries as quickly and efficiently as possible. We must follow dietary and nutritional guidelines suitable for type and lifestyle. All the while getting enough sunlight to brighten, stimulate and to heal us.

First chakra type reminds us of our one common mother, the earth and of our absolutely vital relationship to her.

## GLANDULAR INFLUENCE

The dominant gland active in this type is the Pancreas which rules digestion and nutrition and plays roles in insulin production and the lymphatic system.

**PSYCHOLOGY & BEHAVIOR**

They are a physical! physical type.(see Appendix, No. One)

Number ones resist new ideas and to change.

Their inclinations toward any movement are slow and periodic.

There is a sense of mystery and depth to them.

They are difficult to read, to see beyond the superficial, especially in comparison with any of the other type's.

Resistant. They are stolid, solid and especially powerful in their resistance. When grounded they are as if their feet and legs were imbedded in mother earth several feet. For other high flying types this is comforting. When positively centered #1s are the model of stability.

This is where their strength lies. They are practical EARTHY.

The First chakra type needs other assertive types to resist, to push against to give them vitality.

Their general outlook on life is naturally negative, dim, difficult, boring and almost anything that happens to them is awful.

Life must be endured because that is the way it is.

They commonly have a belief that their efforts will end in failure and humiliation, so why try.

Psychological blocks they commonly deal with are fear of death and fear of being ignorant.

If they act out or become violent it will usually be based on feelings of insecurity.

Even if the results of their labor turn out in their favor it is a temporary reprieve.

They thrive on the isolation necessary to develop their intense dissatisfaction.

They are generally outsiders in their view of things.

They are reticent to share or to give to others a look at what is really happening inside of them and are an introspective type. This gives them an air of mystery to others.

They tend to reflect those around them without revealing their feelings. Just because they go with you or agree with you does not mean that this agreement accurately reflects what they think or feel.

Childish sense of humor.

Perhaps laughing or giggling inappropriately, and if you were to ask them why they would not be able to explain to you the answer.

Prefer not to be noticed . and if you walk into a room full of people they are the ones you either will not notice or will notice last.

May be brusque in defense as to their inability to open up to a more acceptable social standard.

They love to hide and to work in secret. Everything is a personal and private matter to be held closely.

Shy and suspicious of any attention and usually for a good reason. Why would anyone really be interested in a shy, passive, introspective, negative, and potentially dark and moody person? Certainly it must be because there is something that you want from them or to take from them.

When out of balance they are easily upset and could run to the extreme of violence trying to enforce their will or to forestall or prevent a change.

Their suspicion can lead them into fits of rage and anger from fear arising out of their mistrust.

Black and white view of the world. There is no middle ground, no gray areas, or compromises. There is no ambiguity. If it is not good it is bad. This is irrefutable according to their logic.

May be moody. Look at the prevailing Moon or Lunar cycle two days before and two days after for evidence of this. The tides within are reflected in the mind as creativity or lunacy. Emotionally we see them as moodiness, mood swings, or flipping. Their moods swing from childishly giddy to outright depression. This giddiness or the rapid swing or flipping to the depths of depression will catch your attention. Their mood swings will not be affected from within or without. These internal tides may also be observed as certain kinds of sensitivity or inclinations toward sensitivity. This would include symptoms of so called PMS which are seen in men as well as women.

Although women may be more susceptible due to their "watery" nature. Both first and second chakra types seem affected by this watery periodicity.

For many people they will be difficult to work with or to handle as they are especially obstinate. The harder you push them and all argument and persuasion is pushing; the harder they will resist. Like a creature which can dwell underground they will entrench themselves literally burying themselves in their position.

Just because they go along with you or agree with you does not necessarily mean that this is an accurate representation of what they really believe. They can be very deep and profound.

When of an unbalanced nature they can be seen with a disturbing kind of earthiness. I am thinking of particular derelicts and their urban counterparts the proverbial wild man or woman. They may also demonstrate, when in a negative or unbalanced state poor self esteem and a sense of not being connected to the earth.

All of the chakra types have their complex and eccentric variations, however, the First Chakra type is most surely an eccentric type.

They can be intensely and fiercely loyal or supportive. They are tireless in any purpose or cause which has gotten their attention. If you are being assailed or criticized your first chakra friend will not abandon you even to the bitter end provide that there is one.

Women appear shy and definitely do not want to attract attention.

Never quits

Tend to keep their promises.

They are likable. We want to protect them, to dress them better, to help them to open up.

They are cool.

Karmically they seem born to work out the day to day life of a natural man or women, the ordinary person. Every thing about them supports the view of their mission in life.

In difficult times they shine as their traits become the source of tremendous strength. When faced with a hardship they will remain stable. When others are literally thrown about they will remain relatively unperturbed. This is not much of a surprise as they knew beforehand it was going to be rough or they expected the worst. Their aloofness and natural state of detachment may allow them to function in a courageous and exemplary fashion in an emergency.

They want to reduce things to the lowest common denominator. Like the Moon they are quite reflective.

Whether correct or in error they will sound correct and profound.
On a positive side the inclination towards lunacy can translate into a healthy creativity not
limited by practical considerations. Fantasy which leads to creative expression could be an example of this.

They tend to gravitate towards jobs that offer a certain anonymity and little tangible reward.

At least in the external sense. They thrive on intricate and detailed work often to the point of irrelevancy. They are attracted for complex, detailed, circular, elliptical or maze like forms. Think of writing the 101 st. Psalm upon the head of a pin and you approach the idea . They excel in research and libraries, back of the office types processing data precisely and methodically. They are the creators of mazes and labyrinths and have endless energy for this kind of effort. I am reminded of the ancient Celtics and their intricate motifs wondering if they were crafted by the C1's of their day.

Good hunters, they can blend and be still. Their detached state of mind is well suited for this pursuit. Consider of the qualities and attributes of the Roman goddess Diana, a first chakra archetype.

There is an orientation toward issues regarding the basic and practical necessities of life, food, shelter, security. Hoarding treasures, and greed will be evident as one of their principle activities is collecting and saving. In defense of their suspicions that someone is going to take something valuable they will hide and secretly stockpile reserves (like buried treasure!). When balanced this inclination is a boon to everyone around the First chakra type.

They are apt to stimulate a desire for the proper maintenance and security in those around them. When unbalanced their motives and actions will revolve around the material world especially the world of possessions. No thought for tomorrow's consequences` of today's actions.

First chakra types ask the questions upon which our survival as individuals could depend, and leave nothing to chance. Survival of the fittest is a precarious business at best and subject to the whims of chance. The healthy suspicion of the first chakra type seeks to contain and control the riskier elements that are commonly encountered on a day to day basis. This type brings us constructive teaching regarding the conservation of internal and external resources, resources which other types will squander without a moments hesitation.

From the perspective of first chakra all growth is locked in the realm of possibility until fundamental concerns are taken care of. One way or another we must account for how environmental stress affects us.

## CHIEF POSITIVE ATTRIBUTE

Patient. Positively speaking this is a type characterized by persistence and not easily being dissuaded from whatever has caught their attention or otherwise occupies them

## CHIEF NEGATIVE FEATURE

They are greedy and resistant.

## MAXIMUM ATTRACTION

The tall mature looking type that you see them with is a Sixth chakra type. Sixth chakra types are their energetic compliment and physical opposite. Sixth chakra types are the prime or maximum attraction for first chakra types as they are the archetype of everything that they are not. You are more likely to see first chakra female with a #6 Ctype male as the #6 female may find the first chakra male too cool, aloof, and withdrawn.

In combination with each other they are a model of stability and an ideal balance which can lead to growth from childish to mature. This is the ideal model of familial relationships between parents and children. It is particularly significant of the father/child aspect; solid, rational and less than passionate. Though in life few of these relationships bloom or prosper. There is just so much strain and counter strain.

It takes a special kind of understanding to handle the often moody extremes and their negative outlook on life. But to the #6 their childish qualities seem sweet and unprepossessing and are difficult to resist.

We look again to the enneagram to illustrate this relationship most clearly. First chakra represents the beginning of evolution and sixth chakra is the highest in evolutionary process.

In yoga theory of energy movement within the body these two chakras are directly connected with the major highways of the Prana Nadis, Sushumna, Ida and Pingala. These Prana Nadis represent the combined influence of the sun (most male) and that of the Moon (most female).

## REPULSION

No specific repulsion to any particular Ctype is noted.

## CIRCULATION

The direction of circulation or progress for the #1 Ctype is toward the #2 C type.

## HEALTH CHALLENGES

They can be especially tense in the lower back and will carry this tension down into the feet and the legs. As a rule they carry or manifest much of their percentage of physical problems in the legs and the feet. They may also experience difficulty in colon, prostrate, the bones, blood and hair, as well as varicose veins, weak knees often turned in and sore or painful feet with calluses and or bunions.

## LIFE CYCLE of CHAKRA INFLUENCE

The concept of theory of chakra centered body types may also be taken another way. It can be taken as a theory of chakra based Cycles of Life. There are repeating and predictable cycles of increasing and diminishing influence for each principle chakra (see Chart Page 20). For example we are all in a first chakra cycle from age one year (1) to age seven years (7). This first chakra cycle oriented around pure survival repeats at a higher vibration again at age fifty years (50) through age fifty six (56). This system shows the two significant years in which a persons first chakra is naturally in ascendance to be the ages one (1) and fifty (50). You would expect any person to show increased attention and evidence of activity in this chakra at these times. (See Chart Page 20)

# Korosot First Chakra Type: Quick Look

## (EARTH/ ROOT/ FOUNDATION)

Chakra Name- MULADHARA

Ruled By Planet EARTH and The MOON

Principle Element- Earth

Dominant gland- Pancreas

Greek and Roman Archetypes, Artemis, Diana

Desire- For Collecting, Saving, Detoxifying

Nature Is Cool

Introspective, Negative type

Mid-Most Point of Femininity

Stable, Dogmatically inclined

Type under the most laws and restrictions.

Chief Positive Attribute—Patience, Persistence

Chief Negative Feature- Coldness, Greed and Resistance

Obstinate, Stubborn, Passive, Moody

Cool Instinctive Certainty

Immature body, Weak, Timid

Maximum attraction-Sixth Chakra type

Enjoys watery and Dark environments

Scant Body hair

Behaves like an Elephant or Ant

Circulation is to Second Chakra type

# The Korosot Second Chakra Type

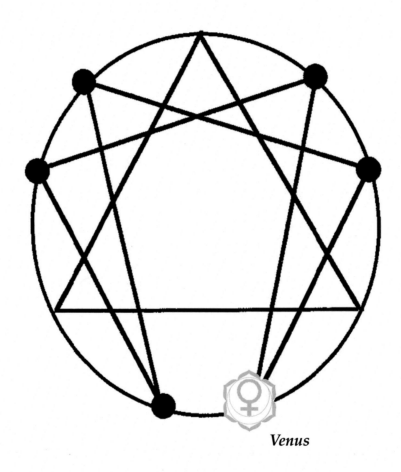

*Venus*

# KOROSOT SECOND CHAKRA TYPE

## The WATER, SEX & SPLEEN TYPE

Aphrodite

## SANSKRIT NAME

The chakra name SVADHISTHANA which means Dwelling Place of The Self

## PLANETARY INFLUENCE

This chakra type is ruled by the planet VENUS.

## ELEMENTAL INFLUENCE

The prominent element observable in this type is **Water.** This contributes substantially to their distinct physical attributes.

## POLARITY& ACTIVITY

Positive, passive, female type. (See Appendix No. Three)

## GREEK& ROMAN ARCHETYPE

The Greek and Roman archetypes for this Ctype are Aphrodite and Venus

# PHYSICAL DESCRIPTION

Tend to gravitate in a group situation to the individual or individuals who will give them the strokes that they need. The more people around them the greater the opportunity to find and to connect with supportive individuals.

Love organized body contact like massage and body work just for the joy of touching. There is a deep sense of enjoyment in the process of giving or receiving physical contact. Anytime anywhere is an appropriate time and place.

Want to always feel comfortable and prefer comfortable surroundings. They wear clothes that would feel comfortable to them.

Wet, steamy, earthy, fleshy

Thick dark hair

They are sensuous and vegetative.

# GLANDULAR INFLUENCE

The second chakras physical attributes are ruled by the activity of the Parathyroid but dependent upon stimulation from the Adrenals found in chakra #5 to actually manifest procreative urges. This partially explains the relationship of maximum attraction between the #2 and the #5 type. This is the sympathetic relationship between the chakras and their associated glands of growth and passion.

# PSYCHOLOGY & BEHAVIOR

Hat-Herut, Hathor

They are a Emotional / physical type.(see Appendix, No. One)

#2's want you to feel better and if they can contribute some physical contact in the process, so much the better. This characteristic is often misunderstood as a desire for sex on their part. This can be a source of misunderstanding as what they really want is to be close, to have proximity.

Receptive in general, able to accept almost anyone no matter how ugly, ill, or unsavory .

Take frequent naps.

They will respond to the neediness of anyone around them; the more needy the stronger the response.

Complete lack of discrimination, which can be characterized as a form of acceptance without judgment.They can be victims of their own goodness without discrimination to protect them.

Second chakra types are like a force of nature in the way that people are not really good or evil to them. People are just people who are to be accepted the way that they are found. This unjudging acceptance places them in close proximity with nature where beauty and beasts coexist in a natural fashion. Nature makes a beautiful coastline; the coexistence of land and sea. However, upon closer examination others see the waves crashing and breaking apart the land.

They feel asking a discriminating question is cruel behavior and unfair.

They are excessively open and generous. Sometimes they are too open, and often have difficulty establishing and maintaining boundaries. Usually, their boundary issues will be on the passive side, as in being excessively passive in the face of unwarranted intrusion or aggression.

Attitude of surrender. Second chakra types know how to surrender, that is to say without reservations. They surrender everything, their home, car, food, clothing, time, energy, attention, and resources go to anyone who can get in front of them and either ask for these things or simply appear in need. In other words, if they have it, you have it.

The only true interest that they might have tends to be of a temporary nature as they will always give their interest up or sublimate it in favor of someone else's. This is not stressful for them. Rather, they genuinely worry if they have considered and given enough or whether they could possibly give more. This often leads to an exhaustion of their resources, external and internal. Not only is this process wherein they allow their interest to be subverted or sublimated not a cause of stress for them, they may not even know that anything of note in this regard has occurred. For example: The #2 type was engaged in and leading a conversation. They are clearly interrupted by someone else with a completely different conversational agenda and do not even realize what has occurred, forgetting that they had a point to make. This example provides of the barest frame to demonstrate this tendency. This tendency cannot be overstated.

#2's GO WITH THE FLOW. They are truly non- linear thinkers.

#2's ideas of success often are pictured with them being next to someone else who is accomplished, famous, and or successful.

They avoid being assertive.

They also void making decisions and would genuinely prefer that someone else do it for them, even if it goes against them later.They will struggle with simple decisions, what to do now or perhaps what to do first or next.

#2's do not like to be alone. They thrive on the stimulation of other more active types and diminish without it. Without this stimulation they appear dull or sluggish.

Need contact, physically and emotionally. Second chakra types are the most sensual. They live for all the hugs, kisses, pats, squeezes, and cuddles that they can acquire. They need to be touched and to be near someone all of the time. Crowds and mobs of people are quite okay.

They touch everything and everyone. It is irresistible to them. A #2 will touch the plants, furniture, animals, and any fruit in the house. If they can see it they want to touch it.

They require little else from those around them. Because of these above inclinations coupled with a lack of discrimination they may be taken advantage of quite easily bother more active and self centered types.

Chances are that a #2 will never interrupt you or overly disagree with you.

Because of their purity of motivation and their obvious receptiveness, #2's are our confidants. We can and do tell them everything as they receive everything with warmth and without judgment or opinions.

They lack independence and independent focus.

They are warm but can be frank.

The basic being of the #2 is in the **Creative Reproduction** of being.

Sex is a thread winding throughout their being. It is for the sensuality of it, the play of it. The stimulation it gives them. There is no inclination to conquer or to control another. There is no using or abusing. Sex is just the greatest way for them to surrender and they do. It gives them everything that they need. it gives them the fullness of the feeling of skin to skin and whole body contact. They can completely immerse themselves in the sexual union in a childlike and joyously uncomplicated fashion.

When negatively centered, or when this sex function is malfunctioning the #2s uninhibited expression of the creative potential in their sexuality is lost. Their energies are then exhibited in inappropriate ways. These tendencies will surface in the form of excessive sexual fantasies and or suppressed sexual urges or desires, leading to frustration or the acting out of frustration, hysterics, tantrums, depression or vacuity (going empty). At the very least there will be tension regarding the lack of proper expression and the satisfaction of good healthy sex.

The #2s inclinations toward romance tend to be based on eros, as their emotions rule their behavior. Conscience and consciousness can be left behind or easily put aside. On the other hand, this orientation may be a powerful and important aspect of how the passive #2 attracts and holds the attention of more active types long enough to develop a relationship. Their steadfast, slow blossoming nature eventually allows for well founded growth and balance to come to fruition.

They have the power of passivity and constancy.

They are steady and can stick to what they desire. Over time this steadfastness demonstrates itself as a tremendous strength. This is like the vine which eventually crushes the wall it climbs toward the sunlight or a tree which grows up through the stone or concrete over time.

Slow and natural growth.

#2*s are natural gardeners and you will often find them in the garden or leaning over a flower pot. Their house would be a jungle if they could arrange it. The evidence is in the way plants respond to them. The plants love them.

They treat children like their plants and are nurturing and supportive of children, forgiving everything.

They love to play.

Once settled in a home or a job they get comfortable and settled. It will not occur to them that somewhere else might be better.

#2's see the logic in everyone else's argument.

They are easily forgotten. You will almost remember them but not quite.

They are the naive type and potential victims of more aggressive types. They want and

sincerely need to belong and this trait is used against them. This is especially true as they are not generally inclined to question the motives or morals of those they care about.

The environment of the second chakra type is always just a little bit unkempt or messy. Think of the classic English garden. In The home there is more attention on the care of the plants than on the more mundane aspects of a clean house.

May appear slothful or lazy to a more active type. But the #2 is not really lazy its just that they have this languorous and slow way or doing things.

In yoga they are ascribed the behavioral characteristics of the **Crocodile** and the **Butterfly**.

Internally, they are inclined to go vacant or slack when left alone or when they are stressed to an extreme. They seem to withdraw to some inner and private place.

They are lovable and huggable.

They are loyal.

They can be found to be firmly entrenched in community organizations, fraternities, sororities, and churches. They are present and notable in all of the healing professions. You will see both men and women of this type as doctors, nurses, massage and body work professionals. They are also notable in the hospitality industry. Many chefs for example are #2's. They want to take care of you and do.
Karmically they seem born to fulfill the roles of the sensitive and supportive types in our
society, artists, poets, musicians, dancers and architects are some examples.

#2 represents the fattening up and the bountiful reserve which is fundamental or necessary for healthy survival. Without #2*s influence #5's are dry, sterile and lifeless.

Since Second Chakra is considered the he origin of personality, the beginning of the social person but immature and vulnerable, then there may be immature and vulnerable aspects to #2's personality.

## CHIEF POSITIVE ATTRIBUTE

Their strongest traits are their purity and receptive nature.

## CHIEF NEGATIVE FEATURE

In their most negative state they literally become non-existent, and invisible. They tend to overcompensate for this by becoming overly attached or even co-dependent.

## MAXIMUM ATTRACTION

Traditionally the ruler of #5 Ctypes, as the #5 is the optimum compliment for a second chakra type.

## REPULSION

There are no strong repulsions.

## CIRCULATION

The second chakra type circulates or progresses to Third chakra influences

## HEALTH CHALLENGES

The kinds of health challenges that #2s have generally relate to their watery, flaccid and cellular bulk. Disorders of the reproductive system and organs, lumbar spine, kidneys and bladder, prostrate and immune system are not uncommon.

## LIFE CYCLE Of CHAKRA INFLUENCE

The important life cycle years for second chakra characteristics for everyone are the ages 8 years through 14 years, and again from 57 years through 63 years. the two most significant years for second chakra influence are ages 9 years and 58 years. (see Chart Page 20)

## KOROSOT SECOND CHAKRA TYPE

### (WATER/ SPLEEN/ SEX)

- Chakra Name- SVADHISTHAN A
- Ruled By Planet VENUS
- Principle Element- Water
- Dominate Gland- Parathyroid
- Greek/ Roman Archetype, Aphrodite and Venus
- Warm, Passive, Positive, Female type
- Desire- Sexuality
- Activity- Fantasy
- Nature- Cool
- Fertility and Fecundity
- Proliferate
- Cellular bulk tending towards plump, Poor teeth
- Watery, May suffer from Edema
- Immature voice
- Chief Positive Attribute- Purity and Receptiveness
- Chief Negative Feature- Attachment and Nonexistence
- Sympathetic, Languorous
- Dull, Sluggish
- Flesh and blood, Earthy
- Sensuous, Vegetative
- Steady, Loyal
- Maximum Attraction- Fifth Chakra type
- Behaves like a Crocodile or Butterfly
- Circulates to #3 Chakra, (Mercurial)

# The Korosot Third Chakra Type

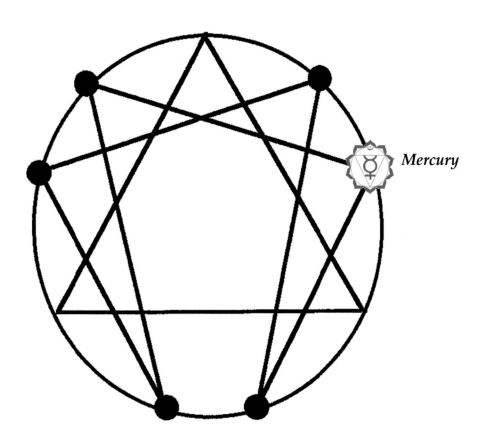

*Mercury*

# KOROSOT THIRD CHAKRA TYPE

## The SOLAR PLEXUS, MERCURIAL TYPE

Hermes, Mercury

## YOGA

The name of the chakra is MANIPURA which means City of Jewels.

## PLANETARY INFLUENCE

The primary planet of influence is Mercury.

## ELEMENTAL INFLUENCE

The prominent element is tire. This contributes to the light, quick and radiant qualities of the #3 type.

# POLARITY & ACTIVITY

Though brighter than the first and second chakra types, #3 is still a negative type. Third chakra type is considered a male type.

The third chakra type is an active and negative type but not the only one. Its energetic nemesis is the male active and negative fifth chakra type. However #3 reveals its negativity in quite different ways. This is due to its relationship to the circulation of the suns energy. In the third chakra the suns energy is in a descending octave, diminishing in brilliance, whereas the fifth chakra is in an ascending octave of increasing brilliance.

This gives the #3 a perpetual dark side. #3 can be extremely self centered and manipulative. They scheme and are devious presenting two faces at the same time, the light superficial one and the dark internal one.

Whereas the fifth chakra type is blunt, direct, and brutal, #3 easily influences others while using subterfuge and trickery. They can and will use their instinctive control of their body and features as an aid to this end. A contemporary magicians act is typically a third chakra play. The right hand does not know what the left hand is doing. You are directed to watch the magician's face and laugh not knowing all the while that your pocket is being picked. (See Appendix, No. Three)

## GREEK & ROMAN ARCHETYPE

The Greek and Roman archetypes for the third chakra type are the deities Hermes and Mercurious.

## PHYSICAL DESCRIPTION

The head and the face reflect the activity of the third chakra. The third chakra rules expressions possible for the face and consequently the faces role in expression of personality. From the earliest age we learn to read, interpret and express all of our selves in communication with other people through expression. We speak of various looks as having a particular meaning, i.e.: sad, happy, lost and so forth.

#3's are especially in tune with this process. They are intuitively facile in expressing and in interpreting expressions of all kinds.

Thick hair, bright eyes and even teeth.

Though physically they tend to be small and slight of frame their strength and power is surprising.

They are lean and hungry in the mind if not the body.

## GLANDULAR INFLUENCE

The dominant gland is the Thyroid emphasizing their role in control of movement and the moving function. Especially voluntary functions and muscles which can be influenced by intentional act of will.

## PSYCHOLOGY & BEHAVIOR

Thoth, Toth

They are an Intellectual! Physical Type, the highest intellect of the terrestrial self or of the earthly mind. (See Appendix, No. One)

#3's are very active and mobile. They can go where the action is and would not think of being left out.

They are often noted for their worldly vision along with great facility of intellect and potentially equal facility physically. Quickness is their domain. They are quite witty and will react quickly to most stimulus.

#3s are the opinionated type full of likes and dislikes. All of the type have certain opinions they are fond of but the #3 is most happy when expressing them.

They are perceptive, because of their energetic ties with the sun. There is much light which keeps their perceptions keen and sharp. They are the highest example of the terrestrial based intellect and the earthly mind. They are in control of their emotions and exude personality.

They want and need to be seen.

They are restless and inclined to move and to have a lot of movement around them. Much like the ring master of a circus, or a master of ceremonies.

Dressing for attention and impact, the #3 will make sure that you will not miss them or mistake them. They would be offended if you did either. Compare this with the first chakra's inclination toward camouflage. They love to glitter, to sparkle, and to catch every eye. They thrive on being the center of attention and will posture like actors to get it. #3 types are natural actors.

Their principle desire is the desire for achievement and immortality. They have a strong drive even to the point of lust for power, fame, notoriety, and glory.

They are cocky and self assured and perfectly willing to announce their sense of their own perfection to the world, or to manipulate someone else to do it for them.

The natural salesman. They can be terrifically persuasive and animated. Its not just that they will manipulate us, they are fun to watch and we will be thrilled by them. Their wit will make you laugh but keep clear. It's all part of their game. Also, at a moments notice this fine and sharp wit can turn aggressively negative and depreciating at a moments notice. It will cut you apart without mercy. Unlike the #2 who is blessed or cursed with virtually no natural sense of discretion, the #3 is abundantly supplied with a keen and sharp discretionary skill. They are like surgeons deftly able to separate the non useful from the useful.

Unlike the #2 type who is blessed or cursed with virtually no natural sense of discretion, the #3 is abundantly supplied with a keen and sharp discretionary ability. They are like surgeons deftly able to sort and to separate the non useful from the useful.

Power, anger and manipulation are their chief negative features.

#3's must have the last word. They will die to have it. #3's settle accounts, hold grievances long and will get revenge. Think of Mafia and Cosa Nostra, Gangs and the like.

When negatively or improperly crystallized they can be great criminals and find much visceral satisfaction in the complexities of subverting and thwarting the establishment. Conversely you may find a similarly inclined # 3 working more legitimately as a detective or investigative professional. They can catch criminals because they have a keen insight into the complexities of the criminal. Sherlock Holms or Hercule Poirot come to mind.

The problem or challenge with #3 in relation to crime is that they truly believe that they know what is best. They should be in charge and are suspicious of authority. They genuinely think that they are brighter, smarter, and more competent than other people. There is little regard for conventions created and composed from outside. We cannot generalize and say that all #3's are criminals per se as that is a function of specific individuals. However, by reason of the examples cited here we can say that they are more casual with it by inclination. As a type they are less resistant to its influence.

Petty shoplifting, carrying pens home from the office, not paying the parking meter, sneaking into concerts are the kinds of behavior indicative of the #3. This is the person who will use another persons identification to sneak into a class on consciousness development as they feel that they are actually too advanced to have to pay. This characteristic in its many guises is referred to as "Tramp" Feature.

Morally they are relatively immature. There is the tendency to practice what I would call "situation ethics and morals." If it suits them then it is ethical or moral.

Their basic being is in the shaping of being. This means that when correctly centered or positively balanced they bring up the lower chakra vibrations around them and release the higher creative influences of these vibrations. When negatively centered or improperly crystallized their energy and light go toward developing and feeding their "worldly" personality or "false" personality.

They want your adoration and if not volunteered will connive, contrive or bribe a way to get it.

Unlike the passive and negative #1 Ctype who is passively suspicious the #3 Ctype is active and will act out of their suspicions preemptively. they feel that the fact that they have suspicions alone is ample proof and sufficient validation as a cause for action. They will then act out and will feel little remorse for any subsequent consequence arising from their preemptive actions, even if it turns out that they were wrong about their suspicions in the first place.

#3 Ctypes really desire to be in charge and subtlety resent any and all authority except their own. I found a modern example of the stereotype in the TV series, "Star Trek The Next Generation" and "Deep Space Nine". The character of the Ferengi is a classic depiction of the third chakra physical and psychological type.

When having a conversation with a #3 you may have the feeling that you have come to be under interrogation. They tend to pick up on comments that others would find meaningless and banal. Will hint that somehow these things will be held against you.

They are masters of "holding accounts." They can and will keep meticulous records of anything that might or could support or protect them or give them an edge or advantage in some way. The positive side of this, is that they show us the strength and conviction necessary to remain true to oneself. Compare this to the relatively wishy washy #2 Ctype.

They are spontaneous and electric.

They always have options and are optimistic that their plan will succeed.

Being natural impresarios, they have much delight in organizing an event or party. Orchestration and coordination of many different but related tasks that would drive another type nuts but excites and stimulates the #3.

Their deepest fear is of loosing control. They automatically become fearful in situations or circumstances where they have limited or restricted input, assuming right away that the result or outcome will be unfair or abusive to them.

They can assume the posture of a victim before they actually are a victim in order to begin to develop and put into play their defense long before there is a reason to be defensive. The only problem with this scenario is that fear and suspicion without a reasonable basis are not good ground to base a reasonable view of things on. When found in this state, the negative #3 will use their bright intelligence in order to be unreasonable.

They are quick to demand their rights and the explanations of these rights. They are equally quick to interrupt this explanation in progress at the first hint of a question. This is the person who in a loud accusatory voice, will inform you that you are in the spot in the line which they were on their way to, when you inadvertently got in the way by being their first. There is nothing that you can say that will affect the nature of your trespass and should you show any resistance toward acquiescing it will only make matters worse.

It seems as though they are the barter gods representatives it seems. They must and will get the best "deal" on anything that interest them. It is infuriating for a #3 to think or to even suspect that someone else may have gotten or will get a better deal.

As you may have noticed in the characteristics portrayed for the third chakra type so far, they are the most self centered and negative type. They find it difficult to imagine that anyone else could not consider their welfare. There is no concept as altruism where they are concerned. Although, they are capable of helping others if they think that it will somehow be of benefit to them.

Like children when they are happy, they are completely happy. When they are mad, they are completely mad. There is no carry over of the first to the second here. If the #3's mood turns angry or suspicious of you, expect no mercy. At this point they cannot fathom or contemplate that yesterday they were your friend and vice versa.

They are generally in complete control of their emotions especially in front of other persons.

## CHIEF POSITIVE ATTRIBUTE

Their radiance and perceptiveness may be their most salient positive attributes.

## CHIEF NEGATIVE FEATURE

Power, anger and manipulation are the Chief Negative features of the Third Chakra type.

## MAXIMUM ATTRACTION

Third chakra types are tempered by and work well with their natural counterpart the fourth chakra type. #4's tend to open them up and mellow them out, off setting their natural sharpness. #4's encourage sincerity and harmony. On the other hand the #3's wit is endlessly amusing to the warm #4. The #3's negativity brings the #4 more into reasonable proportions. You will often see a wiry dark #3 with a robust #4.

## REPULSION

#3's are the most strongly opposed to and by #5, the fifth chakra type. These two types are the polar opposites of attraction and are the most repelled by or from each other of all the chakra types in this system. Like the north and the south pole of a strong magnet they can truly never mix.

With mutual concessions they may be able to associate superficially but underneath there is a visceral incompatibility. Like oil and water its nothing personal. Throughout the ages of man these two types have struggled as the veritable archetypes of adversity. The #3's cunning subterfuge and the #5 's forthrightness and honesty.

I am reminded here of the events of the second world war and the conflicts between the allied forces led by General George Patton, a fifth chakra type versus those of Adolf Hitler, an improperly crystallized third chakra type. This example clearly demonstrates the global ramifications of relationships between types.

# CIRCULATION

The path of circulation and progressive development for the third chakra types is toward the active male of the Sixth chakra type.

# HEALTH CHALLENGES

The health challenges faced are going to be in the upper lumbar region of the spine, the stomach and digestive system, gall bladder and the liver. The eyes or sight related disorders as well as insomnia and hypochondria.

The unbalanced or dysfunctional #3 will act out their manipulative tendencies and attempt to control others. They will have challenges in the area of self esteem and depreciated self worth. They will try to cover up or to compensate for this. They do not like to be seen in self depreciating states and will do almost anything to keep their emptiness a secret.

Look for floods and breakdowns. They will upset easily or out of proportion to circumstances. Observe if they are seeming dejected, discouraged over obstacles, uncertain, lack spontaneity or vigor for the struggle for survival. These are note worthy as normally they would have handled these difficulties in stride.

# LIFE CYCLE of CHAKRA INFLUENCE

The important life cycle years for the third chakra type characteristics for everyone are between the ages of fifteen(15) years and twenty one (21) years, and again between the ages of sixty four(64) years and seventy (70) years. The two most active years for third chakra influence or activity are at ages seventeen (17) and age (66). (See Chart Page 20).

# KOROSOT THIRD CHAKRA TYPE
## (FIRE/SOLAR PLEXUS/NAVEL)

- Chakra Name- MANIPURA
- Ruled By Planet MERCURY
- Element- Fire
- Dominate Gland- Thyroid
- Desire- Achievement, Immortality
- Activity- Vision, Organization
- Negative, Active, Male type
- Nature- Hot
- Restless, Clean
- Greek! Roman Archetype, Hermes/Mercurios, Mythological Thief
- Lean Body
- Abundant Energy, Quick Movements
- Powerful, Mellow Voice, Speaks Rapidly
- Bright eyes, Even teeth, Thick hair
- May have a mustache or goatee
- Chief Positive Attribute- Radiance and Perceptiveness
- Chief Negative Feature- Power, Anger and Manipulation
- Maximum Attraction- #4 Chakra type
- Third Chakra types are repelled by Fifth Chakra types
- Disposed to Hypochondria
- Behaves like a Cobra or Ram
- Circulates to #6 Chakra, (Saturnine)

# The Korosot Sixth Chakra Type

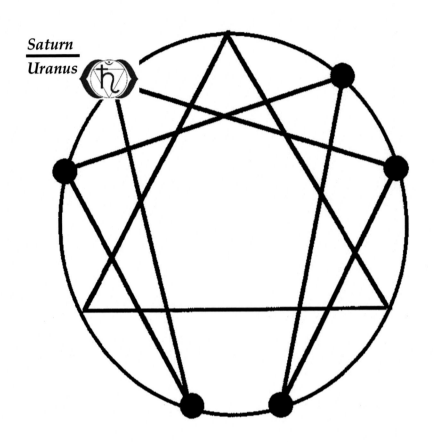

# KOROSOT SIXTH CHAKRA TYPE

## THE THIRD EYE, SATURNINE TYPE

Hera

## YOGA

The name of the chakra is AJNA chakra. The meaning of the name is authority and unlimited power.

## PLANETARY INFLUENCE

The ruling planet is Saturn and to a lesser degree Uranus.

## ELEMENTAL INFLUENCE

The Principle element is Akasha or the mind.

## POLARITY & ACTIVITY

The mid-most point of maleness in the circle of chakra types. (See Appendix, No.Three)

## GREEK & ROMAN ARCHETYPE

The Greek and Roman archetypes are Hera and Iuno or Saeturnus

## PHYSICAL DESCRIPTION

Physically, they are taller than average and tend to tower over others. They have strong, long and well developed bones and may appear a little gaunt. When you look at their face you will see a long head and strong jaw and chin. Their rugged face will tend to have a prominent nose and large teeth.

These described characteristics are more a matter of proportion and symmetry than actual size. Even though they can be lanky like a scare crow; reminding me of Actor Ray Bolger who played the part of the same name in the Wizard of Oz, do not be deceived. They are acutely and finely tuned in their physicality and show a strong natural ability for expression of this physicality. When this happens, they may play the role of an athlete on the one hand or that of a dancer or Fakir on the other. There is a concealed strength about them. Their height tends to belie or conceal their muscularity, unlike other types, like the apparent bulkiness that #5s or #4s are capable of displaying.

This height and strength may give to them an air of superiority, dominance and royalty, which they will likely use to their advantage. Generally you will find them in charge or trying to be. Many presidents, CEO's, and chairmen in politics, clubs, organizations and administrations are #6's. I think the stereotypical diplomat is a #6.

## GLANDULAR INFLUENCE

The primary gland is the Anterior Pituitary, especially regarding its role in regulating the Homeostasis of the body as well as its contribution in balancing the energy of the whole body.

## PSYCHOLOGY & BEHAVIOR

Net, Ptah

They are a Spiritual! Intellectual

Moderation rules with restraint and self denial.

The least spontaneous type.

Unpredictability is a sin.

The right or correct way to proceed is the safest way.

Cool, correct and sensible.

Logical and well ordered, precisely planned. #6 Ctype look at the big picture. They take in every conceivable detail and then organize them into a logical and beautiful whole. This picture is easy to visualize for them. Every new item is neatly placed into the existing structure and there is a place for everything.

Sixth chakra types live according to a previously determined plan, which they will seek to maintain at all costs.

Their perspective on life is that it is purposeful and every day we are making progress forward or progress toward the fulfillment of some grand design. In line with this, their joy in life comes directly from accomplishment and perceived progress. They want to see results in a tangible form. Every part of their life comes under the scrutiny of its relationship to the whole. Every part of their day has a preselected function. The sixth chakra decides everything from the moment that they awake to how many trips to the bathroom are optimal for the day. They are judges by nature, temperament, and inclination. They judge or qualify constantly with an internal set of weights and measures. They tend to classify and divide. Its the process result of the orderliness of the big picture attitude.

They simply want to know who you are and where you originate from, exactly. They wish to know precisely how you are related to them and would like to see a certificate of proof of any claims. This seems to give them a sense of gratification as they thrive on the notion of hierarchy.

The basic being of a # 6 Ctype is the knowledge of being.

Their nature is found in non—attachment and objective knowing.

They are commanding and powerful and rightly so from their lofty height of logic, reason and expansive vision. However far they can see, they can be depreciating to lesser beings who they feel do not share their blessed and lofty perspective.

They are serious and deliberate even in their recreation and play. They are never goofy or hysterical. They are not amused with foolish behavior as their attitude is the very antithesis of foolhardy

They want to know what is the right thing to do exactly. They tend to want others around them to do the right or correct thing from their perspective as well.

They avoid variety as it smacks of a lack of control and chaos and the avowed enemy of #6 Ctype is chaos. A six may eat the same food every day, take the same walk and listen to the same music.

They want guarantees and consistency and are the least spontaneous of all the types. They will never leap or jump at an opportunity or chance. They will methodically work out the pros and cons from every angle before making a judicious choice. After having made this choice they will be able to prove that it was the best possible decision by weight of the facts. Sixes love to refer to the facts.

The sixth chakra type fears immaturity. Premature people, situations or decisions put them on guard. It is a matter of not wanting to move before the proper time; And there is a proper time for everything under the sun. A very sixth chakra way of thinking.

They will spend hours working out all of the various ramifications of anything that they might be involved in. This is fun to them.

Six's are attracted to numbers and to logical thinking. You will find a great number of mathematicians and philosophers of logic among their ranks. That is not to say that sixes can not be artistic. They can be artistic but the thread of logic will show in the heart. I am reminded of the scientist, artist, warrior and philosopher Leanardo Da

Vinci as an archetype of this chakra's energy.

We live in a sixth chakra era today. Every little part of our daily lives are quantifiable. How much education do you have? What is your IQ? your SAT scores; what kind of neighborhood do you live in? What kind of car do you drive? What's the time? Who won the game? The statistics for today are ..., and on and on. From the rating of the restaurant we are going to eat at to our percentage of body fat, we are weighed, counted, surveyed, statistically quantified, rated, numbered and evaluated by ourselves and by virtually everyone around us. There are many ages of man's history where this cataloging of every part of life would have been considered immoral and invasive.

This is the sixth chakra's way of attempting to control all of the unforeseen variables in life, and to eliminate those which cannot be controlled. The fundamental problem for the six here is the inevitable deviation and unpredictability built into the life equation. Six's fear immaturity. They are lost in unpredictability and will many times continue applying time honored measures attempting to control forces for which these measures are no longer appropriate. An example of this could be the way that they are forceful in interpreting and enforcing the literal words of law and code. This is great when these codes are appropriate for the times and the people to which they are being applied, and the worst tyranny when these arbitrary codes and written morals are coercively, improperly or inappropriately applied.

Sixth chakras types, altruistically motivated, may become staunch and tireless protectors of persecuted and downtrodden, may we say, less enlightened peoples. Abraham Lincoln has always seemed to me to be a perfect example of this type in life.

When balanced, the desires of a #6 Ctypes are for clarity, union, unity, realization and revelation or as I like to say realivation! They are humanities shepperds. We find them as our ascetics, Lamas, Yogis, Avatars Buddhas and Prophets. Their natural mastery of abstraction and cool self-motivated discipline coupled with their innate objectivity seem perfectly suited for problem solving, often upon a vast scale. It is not unusual to find #6 Ctypes who have been working for years to find the best way to express a single thought.

Sixes are distant not only from other types but from themselves as well. They may be out of touch with their emotions and can be cold in their disposition. They are capable of receiving important information (which would have others jumping up and down) dispassionately.

There is a religion or a quality of religious expression for a six. This religion would be based on the mind and science. Passion and expressed feelings would be frowned upon as wastes of energy. There would be a heavy emphasis on dogma and ritual for its own sake and their would be little tolerance for new ideas without substantial proof.

As sixes are most comfortable by themselves they would be attracted to disciplines where solitary activity was rewarded. The monks life and monasteries would be especially appealing. As would any discipline which placed a heavy emphasis on training the mind.
Sixes are always full of advise as they always know what is the best way to do anything. They are natural and exceptional teachers and will not hesitate to use any opportunity as an excuse to teach.

Paternal: You know that they can take care of things and this is an attractive quality for them. Although it may not always be true.

They may appear forgetful. The absent minded professor who with patches on his sleeve and cannot remember where he left his shoes and explores the secrets of the universe with his mind as his instrument.

They are likely to correct in a paternalistic fashion allowing for some change over time. They want to see improvement overtime and understand the value of waiting for completeness.

They have the capacity to become real loners, ascetics who move to the remotest possible place to delve into the nature of things without distraction. They walk with confidence the corridors of abstraction and theory where other frail types may fear to tread.

They are the leavening to the bread dough of mankind. They show us when enough is enough.

They can become rigid and inflexible. Formalism may rule, They can get lost in the logistics of thing. These same logistics can become more important than that which they were originally meant to support.

Balance and care.

The nobility of humankind.

The highest order of the worldly progression of types

Historically the British culture was stereotypical of the sixth chakra influence. The stoic Britain and the "stiff upper lip." The British colonial period for example. Also for a time the German culture exemplified the qualities of the #6 Ctype type. In their ambitions to completely control and to
dominate the world for example.

Today we see the same tendency for domination and control under the corporate sponsored, politically correct, plumage " Helping the world to be a better place".

The activity of the sixth chakra type is transformation and transmutation.

The sixth chakra type represents to us the possibilities of synthesis and of relating many unrelated ideas. They are the possibility of living from a place of vision and manifesting that vision in tangible form. They are living proof of the possibility of living a disciplined life.

## CHIEF POSITIVE ATTRIBUTE
The Chief Positive attributes are their openness and objectivity.

## CHIEF NEGATIVE FEATURE
Chief negative feature: Domination.

## MAXIMUM ATTRACTION
The maximum attraction for the #6 Ctype is the #1 Ctype.

## REPULSION
No specific repulsion to any particular Ctype is noted.

## CIRCULATION
The Circulation or direction of progress for the #6 Ctype is toward the #5 Ctype.

## HEALTH CHALLENGES
The sixth chakra type will generally find their health challenges in disorders of the primary gland, Posterior Pituitary, and associated functions. Disorders relating to the homeostasis or of the management of energy resources of the body and of the central nervous system. Bone disorders such as acromegaly. Specific areas of the body that #6s have difficulty with are the forehead, ears, nose, left eye, base of the skull, medulla, face, sinuses, cerebellum.

## LIFE CYCLE of CHAKRA INFLUENCE

The important life cycle years for the sixth chakra type characteristics for everyone are between the ages of 22 years and 28 years, and again between ages 71 years and 77 years. The two most active years for sixth chakra activity are at ages 25 and seventy four. (See Non linear Chart Page 21)

# KOROSOT SIXTH CHAKRA TYPE
## (MIND/THIRD EYE! BROW)

- Chakra Name-AJN A

- Ruled By Planet SATURN and Uranus

- Element- The Mind

- Nature- Non Attachment, Capacity for Self Control

- Desire- Clarity, Union, Revelation

- Activity- Transformation, Transmutation

- Dominate Gland- Anterior Pituitary

- Greek and Roman Archetypes- Hera, Iuno or Saeturnus

- Active, Positive, Ascetic type

- Tall Thin, Large and Long Boned, Long Head, Rugged Face

- Prominent Nose, Large Teeth, Lanky

- Basic Being- Knowledge of Being

- Chief Positive Attribute- Objectivity, Vision

- Chief Negative Feature- Domination and Distance

- Mid-Most Point of Masculinity

- Breadth, Depth and Wisdom, Introspective, Masterful

- Behaves like a Swan

- Tendency to Sit

- Scientific

- Dresses in a Subdued Fashion

- Subject to acromegaly and Bone Disorders

- Maximum Attraction- #1 Chakra type

- Behaves like a Swan

- Circulates to Fifth Chakra type

# The Korosot Fifth Chakra Type

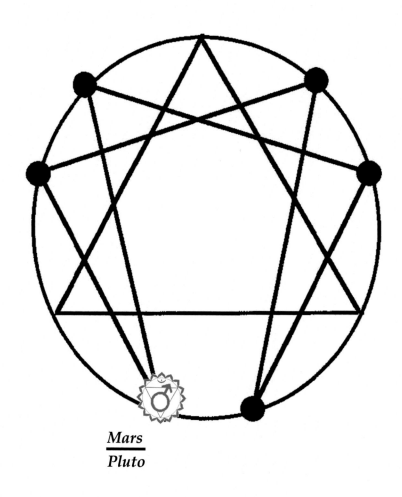

*Mars*
———
*Pluto*

# KOROSOT FIFTH CHAKRA TYPE

## The ETHER, THROAT & MARTIAL TYPE

Ares, Mars

## YOGA

The name of the chakra is Vishudda. The meaning of the name is Pure.

## PLANETARY INFLUENCE

Ruled by the planet MARS and to a lesser degree Pluto.

## ELEMENTAL INFLUENCE

The principle element is Ether. The Quality of the element is unity.

## POLARITY & ACTIVITY

They are Negative, active and male though not necessarily as male as the sixth chakra type. (See Appendix, No. Three)

## GREEK & ROMAN ARCHETYPE

The Greek and Roman archetypes are Ares and Mars.


## PHYSICAL DESCRIPTION

Physically compact, powerful, evenly proportioned, perhaps vivid or ruddy, freckled complexion. They will have an unusual tint to the hair for their heritage. For instance if Scandinavian, in origin, black hair. If Latin, East Indian or Native American, perhaps light, blond or yellow hair. For other heritage you might see red or reddish colored hair. Additionally they will tend to be hairy, both of the face and body. Eyes direct, posture upright and erect. Sharp teeth.

Love physical exertion and if not playing out the role of a warrior will probably be found as an athlete of some variety.

Walk deliberately and forcefully. You can hear them throughout the house. If you see one, you will have no doubt that they are going somewhere. They are incapable of walking aimlessly.

In general, they make a lot of noise. They speak loud, walk loud. and laugh hard.

Their bodies tend to be fit and hard. Find them in Karate and Kung Fu classes. They get high on the thrilling and dangerous aspects of these practices. Find them hanging from cliffs or jumping out of airplanes. They will gleefully bungee cord off a bridge or drive their car exceptionally fast. They are our explorers and adventurers, overcoming obstacles, setting records while pioneering and sacrificing just for the sake of it. They are the Indiana Jones of the chakra types. Sir Edmund Hillary strikes me as a Fifth chakra type. He was the first to successfully mount the peak of Mount Everest. When asked why he had done this extraordinarily difficult and dangerous thing he responded by saying that he had done it "because it was there.


## GLANDULAR INFLUENCE

The Dominant Gland is the Adrenals. Impulse of fight or flight controlled by the medulla and those of rage and pugnacity controlled by the Cerebral Cortex.

## PSYCHOLOGY & BEHAVIOR

Horus, HERU-BEHUTET

They area Spiritual! Physical type. (See Appendix, No. One)

When properly channeled their passion leads the #5 to be the most expressive type, excelling in communication. In some traditions the third chakra also is attributed this characteristic of excelling in communication, especially because of its ruling planet Mercury. However when I say that the #5 excels in communication I mean it in every way. They are consumed with self expression or the communication of the self. True, the third chakra type is a good communicator, but, there is always the tendency or inclination to withhold something, to keep something back intentionally. The inclinations of the #5 are quite the contrary. 'They"re to not hold anything back what so ever!

Their Basic being is the Resonance of being

The warrior

Blunt, direct and brutal.

Passion leading to violence

Passion always in lower types leading to an outlet against other men.

All types grow passionate and quarrel. For example, instinctive types will fight over food or sex. Emotional types will fight over religion or justice. Intellectual types who pride themselves in their lofty and elevated stature will fight over science, theories and abstractions.

The passionate reaction of men and women to and against other men and women only propagates more of the same. It is illusion to blame another individual, faction ideology, religion, cause or country for responsibility. All of us regardless of type are individually responsible for our part in it. The little wars that we endlessly propagate within ourselves and with each other are the ultimate origin of the big ones.

Having seen that as individuals that we are responsible, we must just come to the realization that no one is responsible, such is the nature of the mechanistic state in which we find ourselves. We are responding constantly to influences to vast and numerous to elucidate. The way that anyone reacts, the timing and the scale of their reaction is a product of celestial tension or relationship and the state or level of being of the person at any particular moment. The dynamic of the relationship between all of these things is such that there is constant flux giving us what the ancient Chinese called the Ten Thousand Things.

The lesson here is that when the passionate nature of man ceases to be directed at other men will man be able to free himself. Improbable, impossible perhaps to not fight with others but better to struggle with the real resistance to an individuals path toward consciousness, mechanicality. This is a keen issue.

The #5 Ctypes negative tendencies are transmuted by their becoming invisible. Purification and detoxification are examples of real war if taken on a different scale. For example, an individual might feel that getting rid of an intestinal parasite is good but what of the life of the parasite which is minding its own business ? This may seem to be a ridiculous example granted. However it is only ridiculous because of the disparity of scale between our level of perception and that of the parasite. The fifth chakra type fulfills a natural, healthy and vital role, position and function. As with all of the other types. The trick is to work according to the highest principle which can be applied. As far as ego goes, what about the ego-less and disappearing #2s? A little ego can be stimulating to a relatively more lethargic and less than active type.

Fifth chakra types do not enjoy conflict, they are conflict. In battle they come alive and can fully express themselves even to the point of joyous abandon. There are numerous examples of #5 s while within real battles laughing and singing all the while. This is incomprehensible behavior to other types. There are also numerous examples of #5 types who understood and had a sophisticated understanding of the naturality of the force they represent. I think of the Samurai of Japan and their warrior code of Bushido, '

The way of the warrior is he resolute acceptance of death. The Samurai also practiced the cultivation of what is called Mushin, or No —Mind. The nature of the optimum mental state of the warrior is void. The cultivation of Mushin, No—mind, void and Non attachment allow one to actually be present in the moment, free of non real distractions. This mind set allows freedom from all distractions from the present moment whether internal or external. This being in the moment allows for the possibility of true exchange and communication.

A good example is found in the Bhagivadgita as translated by Swami Prabhupada. It gives a descriptive account in which the warrior Arjuna finds himself on the battlefield. He is assigned by duty to do mortal combat with his own relatives. He begs Lord Krishna to be released from his regrettable obligation. Lord Krishna responds by saying' Realize that pleasure and pain, gain and loss, victory and defeat are all one and the same: then go into battle. Do this and you cannot commit any sin.

War, combat, fighting, altercations of any kind always have been and always will be a litmus test of a persons being. Altercation and struggle with destructive tendencies may be like the test of sex, showing precisely where you are. Fifth chakra types bring to themselves and to all of the other types the dilemma posed by our ability to consume and to harm ourselves and those around us. Resolving this dilemma is the prelude to tremendous opportunity.

The fifth chakras comfort and even thriving demeanor in war and violent situations is not all bad though. If you are in a situation in real life where you need actual physical protection then #5 Ctypes are what you need! Let me give a graphic illustration from a life situation. A #5 Ctype acquaintance of mine who happened to be a tactical officer with a local police department responded to a situation. The situation was one involving hostages.

What had happened was that a gentleman distraught over being fired from his job had returned to his place of business with several firearms. This man went into his supervisors office and shot him dead. He then proceeded to walk around the office shooting at random. Eventually he captured an individual woman and barricaded himself in an office. There was exhaustive negotiations with this man over a period of many hours to an unsuccessful end. He indicated that he was going to kill the hostages and then commit suicide. The psychologist on the scene feared that he was actually going to do a he indicated and made a desperate decision to try to save the life of the women. My #5C type friend volunteered to go in and rescue the women and in fact did so. He was fired upon several times and was able to regain the women's freedom in spite of this. Later he asked me to participate in a ceremony honoring the deceased assailants spirit. This is very five like. #5's can be fearless and respectful at the same time.

This was not an isolated incident. My friend neither knew the woman, nor her assailant. He has been decorated for bravery of this kind many times over many years. This is an example of a #5C type wrestling with flesh and blood. However, #5s also wrestle with powers and principalities.

The physical act of resolving external aggression is analogous and a metaphor to the inner and spiritual resolution of internal conflict. There are examples of mastery of these qualities in life as well. His Holiness The Dali Lama is a genuine warrior and balanced example of a fifth chakra type in his present incarnation. Literally his whole life has been consumed with the issues of conflict resolution and the nature of peace.

Qualities of design that #5s are attracted to are pointed or with points.

Represent the fullness and vibrancy of power when actively expressed. They can be violent.

Can be effective.

They course with the fullness of their energy whether at the head of an army or dealing with purely internal considerations. You have to give them this, they are intense.

Will crash into parties, conversations or other persons with equanimity.

Push the chest out, spread the feet and look or appear ready for anything and probably are. This is not posturing. #5 Ctypes will spend their whole life perfecting skills and attributes necessary in order to be ready!

Their issues are present and important now.

They may control your attention by starring.

They are easily upset or made angry and irritated.

If you make a #5 mad do not worry whether you will know it or not. You will know it right away.

They are simple, direct and tend to work from a well organized plan.

Fierce pride and loyalty. Honest and forthright.

#5's want to do something now and it is difficult for them to be intentionally aimless, even for short periods of time.

Natural military types. They thrive on the regimented environment and excel within it. The consummate warrior, like a fish in water.

They like to play as hard as they work or fight. They may drink or do drugs to excess often to the point of putting themselves into a stupor. Perhaps this is one free moment from their drive and relentless pursuit of honor, perfection and success.

The women, usually Tom boy types when young, grow out of it into competent and powerful achievers.

#5's love logistics. The working and sorting out of the best ways to do anything or to accomplish anything. They are practical and astute. They are essentially pragmatic and realistic about the pro and con of what is in front of them.

May want you to prove your loyalty before trusting you. They first question in their mind is whether you are friend or foe. They do not understand the concept of neutrality and are uncomfortable with those who practice this philosophy. They are especially uncomfortable with the idea of someone without principles. They value direct speech and action. They fully expect that you should do what you say that you are going to do.

Tend to spend a lot of time and energy putting out tires.

#5's work at everything the same way- to conquer it. This holds true whether it is in the writing of a book project, tending the garden, or cleaning the house. Lets get it done now.

They live in the NOW. Now is the best time to do anything and they can do it now.

They will not quit until whatever task consumes them is complete.

Drawn to extremes. When not excited they can be dull and listless. They need obstacles to overcome.

When threatened they will overcome by whatever means available to them.

Look for them on the front line of the resistance, the protest march, the rally, the hunger strike or anywhere they can confront their perceived opposition face to face, Mano e Mano( Man to Man). I am sometimes reminded of the Green peace guy in the zodiac dingy, hand cuffing himself to the anchor chain of the whaling ship. A very #5Ctype kind of thing to do.

#5 types do not contract for their new home they build it with their own two hands.

In conversations they may be provocative, trying to start something. When sensing any weakness they will zero in like a dive bomber going in for the kill. Have now drilled verbally their wife, boss, neighbor or friend into the ground they may be equally dejected at having done so. They want to interact, to communicate in every way possible not necessarily to hurt or to harm anyone. They expect for you to reciprocate in kind and are either disappointed or disgusted when you do not. They definitely want to be taken seriously.

They will try to shock or to provoke you to see what kind of animal that you are.

They may also run away and hide or sulk, pouting, when they feel unfairly attacked.

Love to stand on principle. Any principle will do as long as it was their idea. Do not think that seeing the #5's point of view will help or make them happy. It will not . It will only serve to prove your lack of principle, your lack of guts. You may only get respect as a loyal friend and allay or a worthy opponent. If you change sides they will only think that you are weak.

#5 chakra types are sexually active. Other than in the act of fighting their greatest outlet for tension may vary well be in their sexual expression. Basically they think that they will die if they do not have enough sexual release. Without sexual release they will go into a funk. The combination of sexual energy! frustration and vitality may partially explain to some degree their orientation towards violence.

#5 's thrive on discipline and make it work well for them.

Examples of their intensity can be found anywhere even in the arts. Beethoven composing and playing his bold and strident symphony's.

#5's may become depressed but all it takes to get them up and going is a good challenge.

## CHIEF POSITIVE ATTRIBUTE

The vitality and adventure that #5 Ctypes bring to everything that they are involved with are their best attributes.

## CHIEF NEGATIVE FEATURE

The Chief negative features of a five are ego and destruction and they can be quite violent when negatively centered. However, please note that ego and destruction are not necessarily bad.

Destruction per se is a natural process and only when tainted by negativity such as with greed, hatred and cruelty does it become criminal.

## MAXIMUM ATTRACTION

Their maximum attraction is to the second chakra type. The second chakra type is a perfect foil and receptive partner for them.

They are sometimes found as mercenaries.

When positively centered their energy is geared and directed to truly help others. Many #5C types are found in the roles of Teacher, Sage, Guru, Scientist and Physician. They help and they communicate faithfully as the natural leaders that they are.

## REPULSION

They are also perfectly repelled by third chakra types usually reacting with annoyance and suspicion to them.

## CIRCULATION

The path of progress for the fifth chakra type is toward the heart. Fourth chakra development holds the keys to soften, warm and balance them.

## HEALTH CHALLENGES

They show symptoms of their stressful way of life, suffering from High blood pressure, Headaches, Back and Neck pain, TMJ (Jaw and Cranial Dysfunction) and may grind their teeth.

The kinds of health challenges that #5C types face have a lot to do with their temperament. They are a volatile type susceptible to stress and the harmful effects of chronic stress. This is especially true when they do not have functional outlets for all of their energy. Tension, muscle spasms, headaches are all common. The chief parts of the body or areas of the body to be concerned about are the head, neck and jaw, throat, voice and lungs. There may also be cause for concern with blood pressure, sodium and potassium metabolism, and reproductive dysfunction

### Life Cycle of Chakra Influence

The important life cycle years for fifth chakra characteristics for everyone are the ages 29 years through 35 years, and again from 78 years through 84 years. The two most significant years for fifth chakra influence are ages 33 years and 82 years. (See Non Linear Chart Page 21)

## KOROSOT FIFTH CHAKRA TYPE
## (VOID/THROAT)

- Chakra Name- VISHUDDA

- Ruled by MARS and Pluto

- Active, Negative, Energetic, Male type

- Element- Ether

- Nature- Void, Seeking

- Desire- Solitude

- Activity- Expression, Communication

- Greek and Roman Archetypes- Ares and Mars

- Hair of unusual color, i.e.: Red or "Reddish"

- Abundant Hair on Body

- Low, Coarse Hairline

- Sharp Teeth, Freckles

- Dominant Gland- Adrenals

- Fight or Flight

- Traditional Warrior, Leader

- Facile Communicator

- Loud

- Courageous, Vigorous, Persistent

- Addisons Disease and Hypertensive Disorders

- Chief Positive Attribute- Vitality and Adventure

- Chief Negative Feature- Destructiveness and Ego

- Fifth Chakra types are Repelled by Third Chakra types

- Maximum Attraction-#2 Chakra type

- Behaves like a Peacock

- Circulates to Fourth Chakra type

# The Korosot Fourth Chakra Type

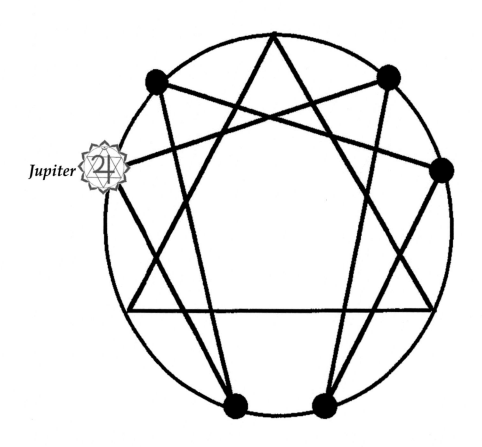

*Jupiter*

# KOROSOT FOURTH CHAKRA TYPE

## # FOUR (4), The AIR, HEART & JOVIAL TYPE

Zeus

## YOGA

The name of the chakra is ANAHATA, which means unstricken or unbound.

## PLANETARY INFLUENCE

The ruling planet is Jupiter.

## ELEMENTAL INFLUENCE

The prominent element is Air.

## POLARITY & ACTIVITY

#4C type is positive, passive and female.

## GREEK & ROMAN ARCHETYPE

The Greek and Roman archetypes are Zeus and Iuppiter.

## PHYSICAL DESCRIPTION

Physically you will tend to see a round face, cheeks, shoulders and corpulent body though not necessarily fat or obese. Their body appears to reflect their internal view of life, full and well rounded. They are short and stout with a large head, scant hair, sometimes to the point of baldness and a Santa Clause nose. Also like Santa Clause they have the inclination toward paunch. Not to be mislead, this cherubic external demeanor may conceal much power and strength. They are not necessarily soft!

Their hair tends to fall out prematurely. It seems, in proportion to the expansion of their mid section. When I see the Chinese effigy of Ho Tai with his rounded countenance, smiling with children climbing all over him, I see a #4.

## GLANDULAR INFLUENCE

The dominant gland is the Posterior Pituitary.

## PSYCHOLOGY & BEHAVIOR

HAPI, Maat, Amun-Ra

They are a Spiritual] Emotional type. (See Appendix, No. One)

The basic being of this type is self abandoning of being.

Regeneration

Is a complex type able to harmonize and blend with all the other types in a positive way.

They are the healing type by nature, the humanitarian. It is within their nature to make well and to bring up the level of energy of those around them. As we are all in need of some kind of healing we all need ministrations at one time or another. We cannot gain access to higher development from a broken or disturbed place. A good beginning is one of health and harmony. #4's help us to get there. #4's teach us that the seed of conscious development may be found within healing.

A loving and gracious type. Their intense nature thrives on love. The experience and play of love challenges and stimulates them.

Their influence provides the emotional stimulus for regeneration that must occur before transformation.

Though a passive type, the first of three moving toward first chakra in circulation, #4 is able to create excitement and to generate enthusiastic participation of those around quite easily. The #4s excitement and joviality is contagious.

#4's are moody and periodic but others easily forgive this in them as they know that they mean well.

They are bored easily and love new things.

Colorful, even outrageous, they can shock you or make you laugh.

It is the most mutable Ctype, allowing and even encouraging give and take. The elemental influence of Air in their nature lends itself to a certain mold ability in adapting to the shape of any environment. #4 Ctypes is similar in this respect to the mutable #2 Ctypes with their water element, but at a higher vibration.

#4 Ctypes are proficient at changing images, pictures and sounds into feelings, and in demonstrating these feelings in a dramatic way. They take instinctive urges, sensations, and impulses toward compulsions and turn them into feelings supported with understanding.

They think big. Big ideas, big visions and large crowd scenes fill their imagination. If they are closer to the first chakra in their development you tend to see a more feminine expression. Remember, the first chakra type is the most female type. This softer feminine version can be flamboyant like a chef, opera diva or musician. If they are closer to the fifth chakra type they will be harder and firmer in their appearance, even to the point of being athletic. I think of heavy duty athletes, power lifters, shot putters and the like.

Love to be noticed.

They do not come and go. They make entrances and grand exits. You can count on whatever is going on to come to a halt when the #4 comes in and greets everyone! The same when they depart in a plethora of hugs, kisses, and farewells.

They like to dress up. They will dress up almost as if in costume. It is very important to them to know what kind of look or image that they present.

Consider the classic Santa Clause as a #4 archetype. Cheerful, resplendent, excessively generous, flashy dresser who loves attention, caring and loving, Ho Ho Ho but watch out because he knows when you've been good or bad. He's got a list and he's checking it twice to see if you have been naughty or nice!

Tend to be wasteful and less than thrifty in material things.

They are maternal and will fuss over and pamper you as much as they love to be pampered themselves. They are open and motherly in their expression as opposed to the paternalistic expression of the sixth chakra type who is very male and severe.

They love to laugh. You may find them in the midst of a group of people on the verge of hysteria, about to fall down from laughing so hard. They love people and the more of them the better. They know everyone, and will have several address books brimming with every kind of acquaintance. They want to stay in touch with everyone.

They love to tell stories and are natural story tellers.

Generally they are reluctant to say or do anything to harm another person. This may reflect their own vulnerability as their own self esteem may be fragile and subject to humiliation. They may defensively pump themselves up with vanity to the point of being seen as pompous. This self inflation can become the root of a crash if the fourth chakra type is found out to be superficially founded. The maxim holds true here, The bigger they are, the harder they fall.

The natural teacher, but one who tends to always be right. This is fine if you are in agreement with them but start asking too many questions or worse, criticism, watch out!

They are sometimes evasive or secretive. There is so much tied up to their being liked and approved by all that they will do most anything to keep a blot or dark part of themselves hidden from view.

When disturbed or out of balance there is an apparent stagnation about them. Their love and care become conditional and manipulative. They will not be able to accept from others. It is possible that they will be moody and that they will become vulnerable and dependent upon the affection of others. Look for unwarranted depression and a general attitude of sadness and melancholy. Additionally they may over compensate for their emptiness by becoming coldly indifferent or even heartless in their outer demeanor.

They are teasers and they are pleasers.

#4s are kind and forgiving. They want you to feel at home and will accept as if you were a family member. They detest suffering and will work hard and long in efforts to help those that they care about or feel responsibility for. They feel responsibility for all under-privileged people.

#4s find silver linings in clouds and are the determined optimist.

If they are unhappy with you they will cut you off. The worst and most heinous punishment that a #4 can conceive of is to be deprived of their company. They will not hesitate to use guilt as a form of motivation and correction.

Theirs is a dark side of the #4 that will manifest when and if they feel threatened.

There is the capacity to be ruthless and destructive.

Very good negotiators who are often seen bringing different sides and factions together for balance, harmony, and understanding. This is when they are at their best.

They inspire trust.

When they are in a good state they can support a large group of dependents, family, friends and others.

They are neither humble, nor discreet.

They are creative and imaginative.

You will find them as patrons of the arts, as they appreciate and love to observe and to collect fine art.

They do move. The juxtaposition of higher and lower influences within them generates the possibility of movement. When consciously motivated, they transcend and rise to the level of first chakra at a higher frequency than before. They progress one step closer to the cul-mination of the evolutionary process.

Their type represents the possible reconciliation of higher and lower influences or energies to actualize the middle, thus stimulating another awareness or understanding that is higher still. Their energy is in the binding, connecting and understanding the connectedness of all things. They want to know every little part of every little part and are capa-ble of extracting cohesive meaning from the most obtuse and seemingly unrelated things.

They are positive with ease and attraction.

## CHIEF POSITIVE ATTRIBUTE

Their chief positive attribute is devotion and generosity.

## CHIEF NEGATIVE FEATURE

Their chief negative features are restlessness and vanity.

## MAXIMUM ATTRACTION

Fourth chakra types are most strongly attracted to #3s. The two of them together are both brighter and more positive.

## REPULSION

No specific repulsion to any particular Ctype is noted.

## CIRCULATION

The path of progress for the Fourth chakra type is toward the earth. Fourth chakra development and progress is in the stability and creativity of First Chakra.

## HEALTH CHALLENGES

The kind of health challenges #4 Ctypes face will be in the following areas. The heart and surrounding area or pericardium, lower lung, chest, breast, thoracic vertebrae, respiratory system and the integumentary system. Look also for recurring trauma or complaints around the hands.

There may be inclinations to problems or concerns associated with the thyroid, adrenal glands themselves and the ovaries. Sexual dysfunction and impotence relate as well.

## LIFE CYCLE of CHAKRA INFLUENCE

The important life cycle years for Fourth Chakra characteristics for everyone are the ages Thirty six (36) through ages Forty-two (42), and again from The ages Eighty five (85) to age ninety two (91). The two most significant individual years for Fourth chakra influence are ages Forty one (41) and Ninety (90) years.
( See Non Linear Chart Page 21)

## KOROSOT FOURTH CHAKRA TYPE
## (AIR/HEART)

- Chakra Name- ANAHATA

- Ruled by JUPITER

- Principle Element- Air

- Active, Positive, Energetic, Female type

- Nature- Intense, Love

- Desire- To Do Something

- Activity- Movement

- Greek and Roman Archetypes- Zeus and Iuppiter

- Dominate Gland- Posterior Pituitary

- Ease and Attraction

- Short, Rounded & Stout

- Large Head, Santa Clause Nose

- Inclined toward paunch

- Scant Hair distribution

- Tend toward Baldness, Poor Eyesight

- Chief Negative Feature- Vanity and Restlessness

- Chief Positive Attribute- Devotion and Generosity

- Tend toward Periodicity

- Maximum Attraction-#3 Chakra type

- Flamboyant, Cheerful, Tolerant

- Depth in Poetry and Music

- Behaves like an Antelope

- Circulates to First Chakra type

# The Korosot Seventh Chakra Type

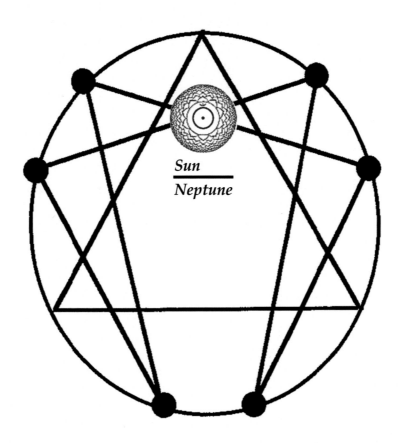

# KOROSOT SEVENTH CHAKRA TYPE

## (The SPIRIT, CROWN & SOLAR TYPE )

Apollo, Sol

## YOGA

The name of the chakra is SAHASRARA, which means Thousand Petaled or Place without support.

## PLANETARY INFLUENCE

Ruled by the Sun and to a lesser degree Neptune.

## ELEMENTAL INFLUENCE

The prominent element is Spirit and its quality is universal.

## POLARITY& ACTIVITY

The #7 Ctype is positive and active though neither male nor female.(See Appendix, No. Three)

## GREEK& ROMAN ARCHETYPE

The Greek and the Roman archetypes are Apollo and Sol.

## PHYSICAL DESCRIPTION

The seventh chakra type is always found in conjunction with one of the six principle types. For example as a 7/ 1, 7/2, 7/3, etc. Take any of the others and add to all of the qualities defining them more sharply both in positive and in negative aspect. They are the least earthly quality in all the various types- unearthly. They are other worldly and sometimes seem to be quite alien. Not alien in a threatening way, but rather alien like Peter Pan is alien in a grown up childish and strange sort of way.

Physically they are fairer skinned than average, with darker hair, wide set eyes that appear large and deep. Transparent, milk and roses, complexion with papery and delicate skin.

Sparse of hair with high foreheads, papery and delicate skin.

## GLANDULAR INFLUENCE

The prominent gland is the Pineal gland and to a lesser degree the Thymus and sex glands.

## PSYCHOLOGY & BEHAVIOR

Ra

They are a Spiritual! Spiritual type. (See Appendix, No. One)

The brightest and most intense of all.

Light seems to shine not just from them but to surround them.

They don't walk they dance.

They are expressive in the extreme.

They radiate.

They appear to live faster than the other types. They seem to run on a different kind of fuel or food or energy. They are obviously not an earth bound type. There is no such thing as a pure type. This rule is especially true of #7 Ctypes types as they specifically do not exist as a distinct type as the previous six types that we have discussed. We find them as a light filled example of virtually any other chakra type.

They will be the most energetic example of whatever type they locate within.

Their most notable traits are speed, excitement, energy, electricity and vibration.

Look at and discover the distinctness of the six principle chakra influences and by process of elimination see the seventh.

They enchant us or bring madness to us.

Their excitement is definitely contagious.

Their proximity to the energy of the seventh chakra and the influences of heaven is imminent for them. Part of them is not here.

They are brilliant in what attracts their attention. They will stun you or blow you away with their brilliance.

We are attracted to them as the moth is attracted to the flame. This attraction is real charisma.

They are always ready or about to cry or to laugh. In fact #7s in a peculiar way are just as child like as #1s, but with infinitely more energy. They may be immature in emotional development. Like children they are sometimes moody and easily distracted.

They do not tend to think in a practical way and are not good for their day today affairs.

They simply forget things like rent, dinner, or appointments.

In the seventh chakra type the circuit and cycle of the chakra influence in mankind is complete.

They thrive for fantasy and tend to live their life as if it were one. They will go to great lengths to live according to the ideal of some fiction that has gotten into them.

They are hopeless romantics and often pine away for unrequited love.

They are the unprepared type for the vicissitudes of life and find much solace in their dream world. These are the master poets of delicate but deep and dramatic sensibilities. I think of Keats, Shelly, Rilke and perhaps Coleridge.

They are the delicate flowers of our species.

The greatest desire of #7 Ctypes is to achieve extended and perfect consciousness, beyond all categories or limitations perceivable, flowing without obstruction as the pure and free manifestation of light. You see this orientation evidenced in their art, music, poetry and sculpture.

They are so tightly wound that simple little things and occurrences that would go unnoticed or would be inconsequential to other types become immense, insurmountable and devastating to them.

They feel that they are special and it should be obvious to you. There is this expectation about being placed high above others as it is their rightful place and at the same time there may be present overwhelming fear and self doubt.

Usually their criterion for selecting friends is who is most attractive or eclectic.

You will see them on the stage or at the opera. Many of them will be painters or artists or musicians and singers. Sometimes Michael Jackson strikes me with strong characteristics of a #7. He certainly is eclectic enough.

Tragic lives and early deaths mark the passage of many #7s.

They are idealistic and generally positive.

They are the least masculine or feminine. It depends more on who they are with as to which traits dominate. At the same time they are intensely sexual. Though perhaps without the clearly delineated roles that the other types tend to follow. Sex may be a valuable outlet for them, their boundless energy has to be expressed one way or another.

#7s are consumed to the extreme with their appearance and spend a great deal of time, effort and money around this issue, more so than any other type.

**CHIEF POSITIVE ATTRIBUTE**

They tend to have perceptions beyond the ordinary.


**CHIEF NEGATIVE FEATURE**

Their immaturity.

**MAXIMUM ATTRACTION**

Unlike the other types #7 Ctypes do not have a maximum attraction.

They are comfortable with every type and will surround themselves with every kind or type. Discrimination is not one of their stronger suits and as a result of this may be and often is taken advantage of by more assertive type, all with little resistance.

They are not defined by the attractions and repulsion's that so dominate and control the other types. Their basic being is purity of being. They are determined to live out their life according to their nature.


**REPULSION**

See Maximum Attraction above.


**CIRCULATION**

The circulation of the #7 Ctype is unknown.


**HEALTH CHALLENGES**

They are not strong in the physical sense and are prone to many illnesses with little real resistance.

The kinds of health challenges that #7 Ctype face will be in the following areas: The Cranium and the brain, the immune system and the Thymus. They may also have eye sight and or vision related disorders. Classically #7 Ctypes have suffered from all kinds of malaise and depression to the point of suicide. When out of balance their innate energy may be thwarted by chronic fatigue.


**LIFE CYCLE of CHAKRA INFLUENCE**

The important Life Cycle years for Seventh Chakra characteristics for everyone are the ages forty- three (43) to ages Forty-nine (49) and again from age ninety two (92) to age ninety nine (98). The two most significant years are the years of Forty-nine (49) and ninety eight (98).(See Non Linear Chart Page 21)

# KOROSOT SEVENTH CHAKRA TYPE
## (Crown)

- Chakra Name-SAHASRARA

- Ruled by -SUN, and Neptune

- Element- Spirit (No classical elemental association)

- Dominant Gland- Thymus

- Nature- Being

- Active, Positive, Cheerful, Youthful

- Desire- Extended Consciousness

- Activity- Transfiguration

- Greek and Roman Archetype- Apollo and Sol

- Immature, Powerful, Intense

- Active, Brilliant

- Fine, Thin Waist

- Fragile, Sickly, Suicide Prone

- World twelve bodyt ype (Ray of Creation)

- Graceful, Wide Shoulders

- Broad Delicate Forehead

- Rosy Cheeks, Long Hands, Fair Skin

- Circulation- Unknown

- Chief Positive Attribute- Perceptions beyond normal limitations

- Chief Negative Feature-Immaturity

- No Maximum Attraction

- Circulation- Unknown

# Appendix No. One

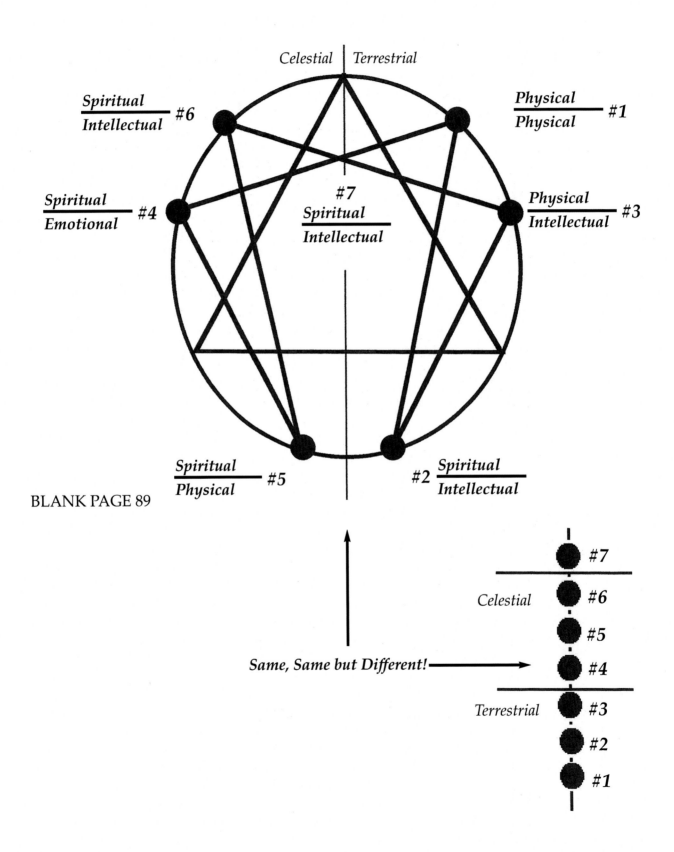

BLANK PAGE 89

# Appendix No. Two

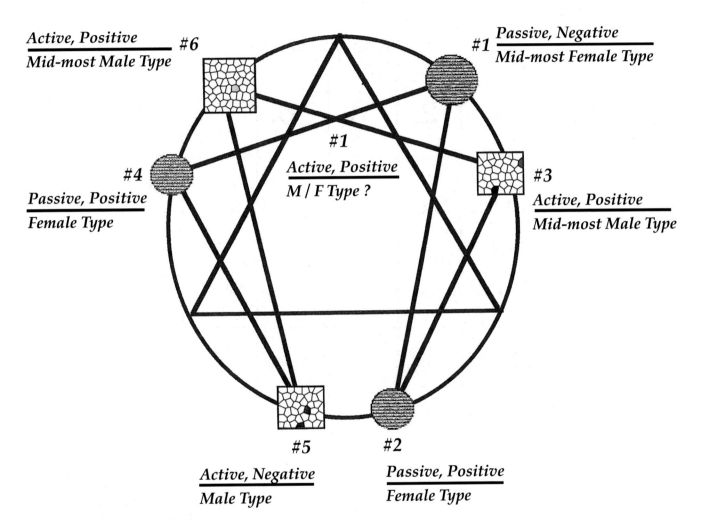

**Enneagram Bodytype Chart
Of
Activity & Polarity**

# Appendix No. Three

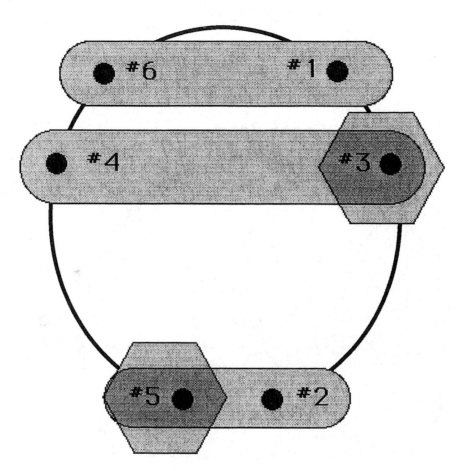

## Attraction & Repulsion

**Three Different Kinds of Social Bondings or Relationships
Revealed when C types Interact.**

**A)** #6's & #1's, The push and pull of familial connections, especially those between parents and children.

**B)** #4's & #3's, Social dynamics outside of the family in the circle of friends, aquaintenances both personal and professional.

**C)** #5's & #2's, The role of passion, disturbing emotions, and the intensity of lovers.

**(#5 & #2: Max Attract, #5 & #3: Max Repulse)**

# Appendix No. Four

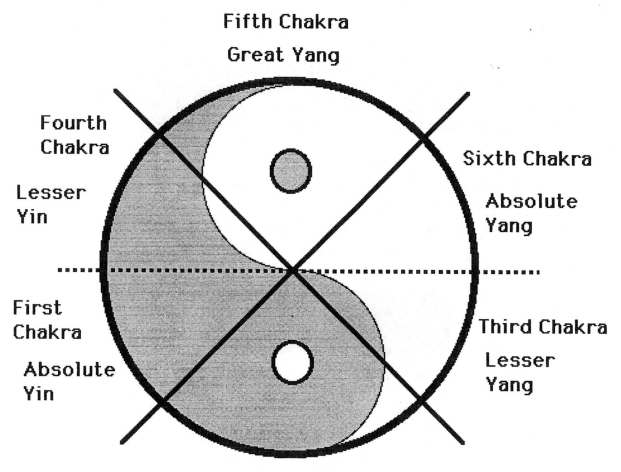

Fifth Chakra
Great Yang

Fourth
Chakra

Lesser
Yin

Sixth Chakra

Absolute
Yang

First
Chakra

Absolute
Yin

Third Chakra

Lesser
Yang

Second Chakra

Great Yin

## Theory of Yin/ Yang
## &
## Chakra Correlations

# Appendix No. Five

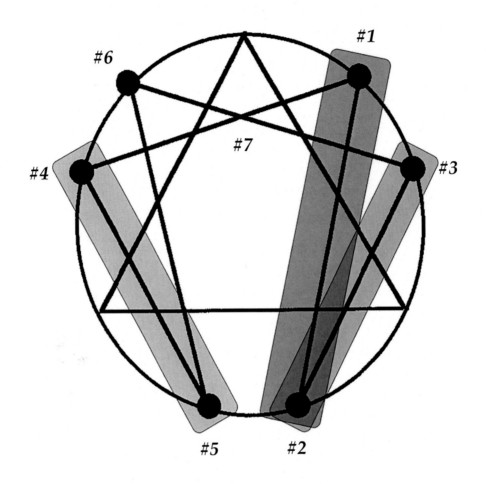

# Chakra Correlations with Three Dosha

| Vata | Kapha | Pitta |
|---|---|---|
| #5 & #4 | #2 & #1 | #3 & #2 |

# Appendix No. Six

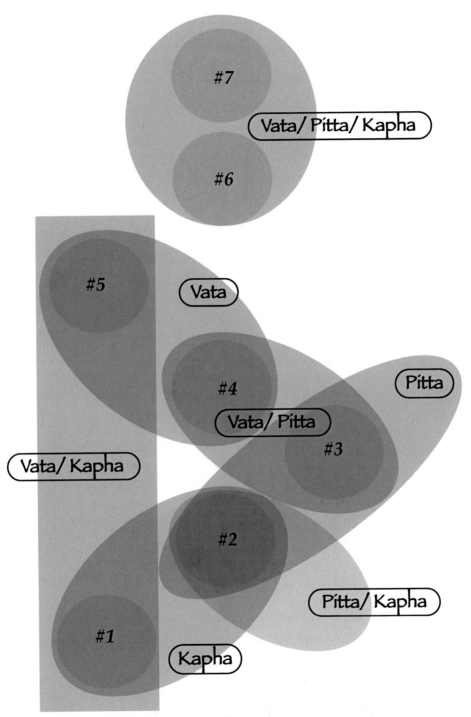

## Seven Types of Constitutions Correlated to Chakra

| Vata | Kapha | Pitta | Pitta/ Kapha | Vata/ Pitta | Vata/ Kapha | V/ P/ K |
|------|-------|-------|--------------|-------------|-------------|---------|
| #5 & #4 | #2 & #1 | #3 & #2 | #2 | #4 & #3 | #5 & #1 | #6 & #7 |

# Appendix No. Seven

## Miscellaneous

| Negative Qualities | | Positive Qualities |
|---|---|---|
| #1 | Stubborn | Creative, loyal |
| #2 | Lazy | Warm, Sympathetic |
| #3 | Restless | Quickness, Agility |
| #4 | Intriguing | Ease, Attraction |
| #5 | Destructive | Courage, Vision |
| #6 | Introspective, Domination | Breadth, Depth, Wisdom |

## FIVE POLARITIES OF BASIC TYPES

**A)** Passive/ Negative (PN)  #1 Ctype

**B)** Passive/ Positive (PP)   #2 Ctype

**C)** Active/ Negative (AN)  #3 Ctype, #5 Ctype

**D)** Active/ Positive (AP)   #6 Ctype, #4 Ctype

**E)** Any of the above plus #7

## OPPOSITES ATTRACT

**A)** Positive, Mature, Male and Parental #6 & #1 Negative, Undeveloped, Female, and, Childish

**B)** Positive, Corporal, Jocular, and Flamboyant #4 & #3 Negative, Lean, Secretive, and witty

**C)** Negative, Extrovert, Physical and Energetic #5 and #2 Positive, Receptive, Emotional and Lethargic

**D)** The Seventh chakra type is essentially attractive to all other principle body types.


## SIMILARS REPULSE

#5 & #3, Aggression, Altercation and repulsion of similars. Instinctive dislike leading to immediate and sometimes violent opposition. Too similar to mistake and too different to endure. Outsiders might confuse these two types with one another as they are both active and negative. Revealing themselves with similar goals but as they are coming from such radically different points of view what they tend to do in life is to collide, like two trains on the same track going in opposite directions.

# Appendix No. Seven

Chakra, Regions of Influence, Glands and Crystals

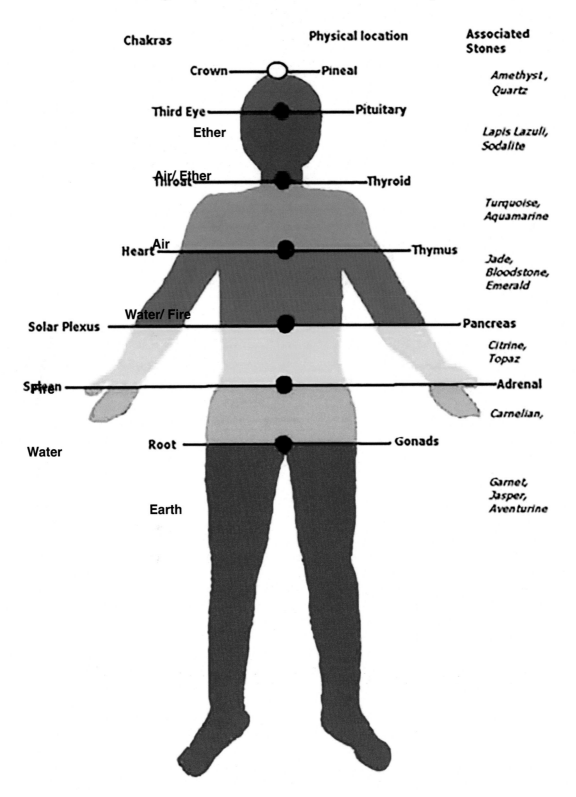

**Chakras**

Crown
Third Eye
Ether
Air/ Ether
Throat
Air
Heart
Water/ Fire
Solar Plexus
Spleen
Fire
Water
Root
Earth

**Physical location**

Pineal
Pituitary
Thyroid
Thymus
Pancreas
Adrenal
Gonads

**Associated Stones**

Amethyst, Quartz

Lapis Lazuli, Sodalite

Turquoise, Aquamarine

Jade, Bloodstone, Emerald

Citrine, Topaz

Carnelian,

Garnet, Jasper, Aventurine

# Appendix No. Eight

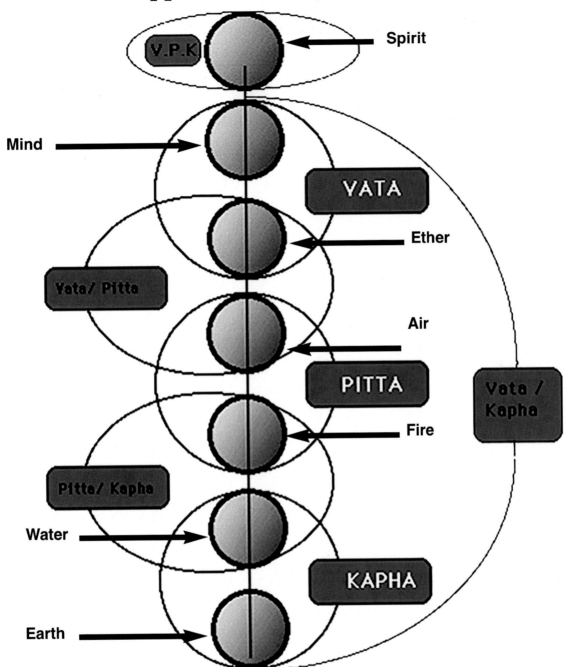

Correlations between Tri-Dosha and SevenChakra

## Three Doshas

Vata | Kapha | Pitta

*4 & 5    *1 & 2    *2 & 3

# Bibleography

Anonymous, *A Point in The Work*, England, Unknown, Authors personal Collection

Blavatsky, H.P. *The Secret Doctrine*. 6 Vols. Wheaton. Theosophical Publishing

Bennett, J .G. *The Dramatic Universe*, Vol. 1. Charles Town WV. Coombe Springs Press. 1956. Revised 1987

Bennett, J .G. *Transformation*. Charles Town WV. Claymont Communications. 1978

Bennett, J.G. *Enneagrarn. Studies*, York Beach Samuel Weiser, Inc.  1963 & 1983

Chia, Mantak. *Chi Nei Tsang*, New York. Healing Tao Books. 1990

Collin, Rodney. *The Theory of Eternal Life*, Boulder. Shamballa. 1984

Collin, Rodney. *The Theory of Conscious Harmony*, Boulder. Shamballa. 1984

Corbin, Henry. *Spiritual Body and Celestial Earth*, Boston. Princeton University Press. 1977

Collin, Rodney. *The Theory of Celestial Influence*, Boulder. Shamballa. 1968

Casteneda, Carlos. *A Separate Reality*, New York. Simon & Schuster. 1971

Cunningham, Scott. *Cunninghams Enclyclopedia of Crystai, Gem and Metal Magic*, St. Paul. Llewellyn. 1993

d'Olivet, Antoine Fabre. *Hermneutic Interpretations of the Origins of the Social State of Man*, Trans. Nayan Louise Redfield. New York. Putnam. 1915

De Mailly, Solange. *Astrology, History, Symbols & Signs*, Vermont. Inner Traditions. 1981

Davis, F.A. *Tabers Cyclopedic Medical Dictionary*, Philadelphia. 1989

Friedlander, Joel. *body types*, New York. Globe Press Books. 1986

Godwin, Joscelyn. *Harmonies of Heaven and Earth*, Vt. Inner Traditions. 1987

Iyengar, B.K.S.. *Light on Yoga*, New York. Schocken Books. 1966

James, Anthony B., *Traditional Thai Medical Massage*, Meta Journal Press, Atlanta, GA, 1984

James, Anthony B., *The Chakra Poster*, Meta Journal Press, Chicago, 1992

James, Anthony B., *Nuad Boran, Traditional Thai Yoga Therapy*, Meta Journal Press, Atlanta, GA,  1994

Johari, Harish. *Chakras*, Rochester. Destiny Books. 1987

K. Ananda. Coormaraswamy. *The Dance cf Siva*, New York. Noonday Press. 1957

Ledbetter, C. W. *The Chakras*, Wheaton. Theosophical Publishing House. 1927

Motoyama, Hiroshi. *Theories of the Chakras*, Wheaton. Theosophical Publishing House. 1981

Ouspensky, P.D. *The Fourth Way*, New York. Vintage Books. 1971

Ouspensky, P.D. *In Search af The Miraculous*, New York. Harcourt, Brace and World. 1949

Paulson, Genevieve. *Kundalini and the Chakras*, St. Paul. LLewellyn Pub. 1991

Phillips, Denning. *Planetary Magic*, St. Paul. LLewellyn Pub. 1992

Rilke, Rainer Maria. *Diurno Elegies and The Sonnets to Orpheus*, Trans. A. Poulin Jr. Boston. Houghton, Mifflin Co. 1955

Rilke, Rainer Maria, *Poems From The Book of Hours*, New York. New Directions. 1941

Sharamon and Baginski. *The Chakra Handbook*, WI. Lotus Light. 1991

Speeth, Kathleen Riordan and Ira Friedlander. *Gurdjieff*, New York. Harper and Row. 1980

## About the Author

Aachan, Anthony B. James DNM(C), ND(T), MD(AM), DOM(C), DPHC(h.c.), PhD, M.Sc., RAAP, SMOKH stands out as the second non-ethnic Thai to be formally certified and recognized as a Khruu or teacher of traditional Thai martial and healing arts. Dr. James is the first United States instructor to receive recognition in Traditional Thai Medical Massage by both US and agencies in Thailand. First to be recognized by American Oriental Bodywork Therapists Association (AOBTA , Instructor Certificate #32) and the Association of Allied and Professional Bodyworkers (ABMP). Aachan James is also the founder of the first international professional association representing primarily Thai Style, Ayurveda and energy based therapist, ( The International Thai Therapists Association, Inc. (ITTA, Inc. 1991-2012) as well as Director of Education of The Thai Yoga Center in Brooksville,, FL.

Having traveled and lived extensively throughout Southeast Asia, he has completed advanced training programs in several different countries i.e. Thailand, India, Philippines, Indonesia, India and China. His Primary focus, however, is and always has been on the traditional Vedic healing arts of Thailand. Dr. James was awarded the prestigious "Friend of Thailand Award" 2002, for development and promotion of Thai classical arts, Thai Massage and Thai Yoga therapies.

On December 1st. 2006, Anantasuk School of Traditional Thai Medicine, Hua Hin Thailand. Dr. Anthony James receives "Aacharn", Master Instructor recognition from the Wat Po Association for Traditional Thai Medicine, Anantasuk School for Traditional Thai Medicine and Wiangklaikangwon Industrial Community & Educational College.

Currently Aachan James is directing the day to day development of the NAIC and the SomaVeda College of Natural Medicine: Thai Yoga Center certification and college degree program. This 20 to over 3000 hour professional development program consists of five levels and supplemental courses. It is complimentary and designed to have parity with other similar certification courses in traditional oriental bodywork therapies such as Shiatsu, Amma or Tuina etc. This program, presented nationally and internationally, is setting a high standard at many schools of therapeutic Yoga around the country.

Aachan James, A Traditional Naturopathic Physician and MD(AM) was a personal apprentice of the 36th GrandMaster Phaa Khruu Samaii Mesamarn of the Buddhai Sawan Institute, Nongkam Thailand. He is a graduate of the Traditional College of Medicine Wat Chetuphon, Bangkok as well as adjunct faculty training program of the Buntautuk Northern Provincial Hospital and Foundation of Shivago Komarpai, Old Medicine Hospital under Aachan Sintorn Chaichagun, Chiangmai Thailand. This book and others authored by Dr. James are currently being used in Thailand to train both Thai and western students. In addition, currently holds Special Faculty Position for several schools in Thailand with formal teaching recognitions from the Royal Thai Departments of Commerce, Trade exports Department and Royal Thai Ministries of Health and Education.

Aachan James was given the award in recognition of his work and contributions in the field of Traditional Thai Medicine and Thai Yoga Therapy. His accomplishments include: publishing the first book on Thai Massage in the english language "Nuat Thai, Traditional Thai Medical Massage", Meta Journal Press, 1984. Becoming the first licensed Thai Yoga and Thai Massage practitioner in the United States (Dekalb County, GA 1984), The first recognized Thai Massage Instructor in the US, (AOBTA: 1990 Member #37).

For more information on programs developed by Aachan J, visit WWW.ThaiYogaCenter.Com
For more information on books, DVD and educational media visit WWW.BeardedMedia.Com

96801194R00095

Made in the USA
Lexington, KY
23 August 2018